G000275889

THE BANTING BAKER

LOW CARB HIGH FAT TREATS

The recipes in this book were developed in the
Primal Chow kitchen – see www.primalchow.co.za

Published by Jacana Media (Pty) Ltd in 2015

10 Orange Street
Sunnyside
Auckland Park 2092
South Africa
+2711 628 3200
www.jacana.co.za

© Catherine Speedie, 2015

All rights reserved.

ISBN 978-1-4314-2266-1

Cover design by publicide
Set in Avenir 10/14pt
Printed and bound by Craft Private Ltd
Job no. 002551

Also available as an e-book:
d-PDF ISBN 978-1-4314-2267-8

Find the Banting Baker:
🅵 Banting Baker Book
🐦 @bantingbaker

See a complete list of Jacana titles at www.jacana.co.za

Disclaimer

This book is intended to share recipes that have been developed in
the gingko and Primal Chow kitchens. While it offers an overview of the
philosophy and rationale behind the low-carb diet, it must be noted
that it expresses the opinions of the writer and is not intended to be
received as gospel. Nor do any of the ideas contained herein purport to
present any definitive medical- or health- oriented 'truths'.

THE BANTING BAKER

LOW CARB HIGH FAT TREATS

CATHERINE SPEEDIE

JACANA

CONTENTS

INTRODUCTION

How you eat is how you live

A big statement perhaps, but in 2003, the Human Genome Project proved beyond a shadow of a doubt that our genes do not cause any of the diseases we seem to be plagued by in modern times. It showed, in fact, that it's not our genes but what they're exposed to that leads to disease, and that includes our food and our environment.

So if you've picked this book up, I imagine that you're already aware of how our nurture, or more accurately in this case, our nutrition, affects our nature. If our bodies are the vehicles that carry us through this journey of life, then it makes infinite sense to keep what we put into those machines as clean as possible. While we wouldn't dream of putting diesel into a petrol engine, we feed ourselves with foods developed in a chemistry lab and then mass produced at the lowest possible cost with ingredients that Big Agri and Big Government have genetically modified and subsidised so that they appear in almost everything you put in your mouth. Whew! Astounding.

I digress but only slightly.

The Low-Carb High-Fat diet, known more colloquially as the Banting diet or the 'Tim Noakes diet', is not just about upturning the food pyramid and thus the conventional wisdom that has ruled for the last 40-odd years. It's about waking us up to what our bodies are naturally 'wired' for in terms of optimal sustenance and body weight. It's about realising that along the trajectory of commercial and industrial 'progress', we've lost sight of our humanness, and moreover our basic biology. In the evolutionary scheme of things, we're still way, way closer to Palaeolithic man than we are to some possible future version of ourselves.

Going back to the wisdom of the past and stripping out the high-density carbs that provide the cheap thrills (but sadly not-so-cheap ills) of our fast-paced, manic lives, and replacing these with slow-burn essential fatty acids delivers us with precisely the kind of sustained energy we need to deal with twenty-first-century life. That said, giving up the chocolate cake ain't so easy. Sweet treats and baked goods are deeply associated with comfort, time out and good times, rewarding us after a hard day's work.

Here's the thing though – one doesn't have to deny oneself these little pleasures. This book will hopefully show you that the low-carb highway is not about denial and deprivation, it's very largely about substitution. Once you've got your head around it, stocked up your pantry with the right ingredients, and armed yourself with a spirit of adventure, you'll discover that you can create the most sublimely satisfying stuff. Stuff your taste buds will quickly choose over the stuff they once considered pleasurable. The stuff of goodness. The stuff of pure bliss. Really.

LOW-CARB LOGIC AKA BANTING 101

As anyone who has followed the press coverage in South Africa around the low-carb diet knows, it has stimulated heated debate, vociferous opinion and tons of controversy, with the medical fraternity still largely on the 'against' side, although this is now changing as more and more data begins to reveal that the logic is sound, and more than that, supported by a substantial body of scientific evidence.

Here we will look at what the foundation of all the fuss is, and at some specific points that are integral to the 'for' argument. First off, a little history to what created the very thing that the low-carb high-fat diet contests – the low-fat high-carb diet!

The lipid hypothesis

In the early 1950s, post World War II, research began emerging that seemed to link foods with saturated fats, like eggs and red meat, to coronary heart disease. Soon a theory emerged, which posited a direct relationship between the amount of saturated fat and cholesterol in the diet and the incidence of coronary heart disease or cardiovascular disease (CVD) and increasingly this began to take hold of medical and nutritional thinking. The theory became known as the lipid hypothesis, and by the 1960s the American Heart Association had recommended that people reduce their fat, and particularly their saturated fat, intake.

While it now appears that many of the studies on which this thinking was based were deeply flawed in many ways, and that *correlation* became confounded with *causation*, by 1976, the US Senate had held a series of committee meetings on the topic of 'Diet Related to Killer Diseases'. In 1977 the Senate issued its Dietary Goals for the United States, advocating eating less saturated fat and more carbohydrates. In 1980 this became further bolstered by the publication of the Dietary Guidelines for Americans, jointly issued by the US Department of Agriculture (USDA) and the Department of Health & Human Services (DHHS). By the mid-1980s the injunction to reduce fat was stronger than ever and by the early 1990s the eponymous 'food pyramid' was released as a graphic that easily conveyed the principles of the 'ideal' diet being one based on different proportions of calories coming from different food groups, with fats right at the top of the pyramid and thus to be used 'sparingly'.

'Sweets' were also listed at the top of the pyramid, interestingly enough, with cereals occupying the lowest, largest category. While the guidelines advocated for more carbs in the form of fruit, vegetables and whole grains, what seems to have happened was that the average Joe took that to mean that *any* kind of carbs were good while *any* kind of fat was bad. Big Agri and the food industry were right there to take advantage of this lack of discretion. High-carb, low-fat foods became the norm with seed oils and elements like high-fructose corn syrup infiltrating just about everything. Once the fat was stripped out, taste was lost so sugar was thrown in to compensate.

The US Dietary Guidelines with their low-fat orientation were issued at around the same time as the American obesity epidemic started, an epidemic that soon spread to other parts of the world. And while we know that correlation does not equal causation, it is highly unlikely that this was just coincidental. And, during the period of the rapid increase in heart disease (1920–1960), American consumption of animal fats declined, but consumption of hydrogenated and industrially processed vegetable fats increased dramatically. (*As an aside, to this day, there is no official limit for sugar consumption in the US. While there is a recommended daily allowance (RDA) for elements such as calcium, total carbs, fat, selenium and all other essential nutrients, it is suggested that people get no more than 25% of their calories from added sugar. Most other governments and health agencies recommend saner, safer limits, with the World Health Organization recommending people obtain no more than 5% of daily calories from added sugar.*)

Along the low-fat highway, nutrient-rich foods like eggs became the epitome of evil, as did any sources of cholesterol, which in fact plays a vital role repairing wounds, as components of many important hormones including the sex hormones and serotonin, and in the functioning of the brain and nervous system.

The notion that eating saturated fat and cholesterol-rich foods will cause cholesterol levels to rise and make people more susceptible to heart disease has now been largely overturned as there is in fact no substantive scientific evidence to link dietary fat and cholesterol to blood serum cholesterol levels and then heart disease. So yes, while elevated triglycerides in the blood have been positively linked to proneness to heart disease, these triglycerides do not come directly from dietary fats – we now know that they are made in the liver from any excess sugars that have not been used for energy.

The carb hypothesis

While the low-fat hypothesis largely won out (certainly in the US, which then dominated global thinking, and until relatively recently that is), there has always been a body of evidence to suggest that it was not the only or primary explanation for the rapid rise in what have come to be called the 'diseases of civilisation'. As far back as the early 20th century, physicians and researchers including the likes of Albert Schweitzer were observing how tribal communities began to show very clear health issues as they abandoned their traditional diets upon exposure to the 'Western' diet, heavy in refined carbohydrates and sugars.

Carbohydrates have historically been believed to be 'essential' as the source of the glucose that fuels the body. But while there are 'essential' elements such as essential fatty acids and essential amino acids, there is no such thing as an 'essential carbohydrate'. Carbs are an easy, quick-release fuel, but the body can obtain sufficient glucose from sources like leafy green vegetables.

Chronically elevated levels of the hormone insulin are arguably the number-one problem we now have as a global society. Insulin's main job is to regulate sugar levels when glucose is present in the blood. When too much glucose is present, a cascade of hormonal responses ensues, with insulin kicking in so that tissue cells take up the glucose from the bloodstream, storing it in the form of glycogen and as lipids (fat). It also impacts cellular electrolyte balances and amino acid uptake. When glucose levels are consistently high, cells become resistant to insulin because they're just overloaded with it. The pancreas compensates, beginning to produce yet more insulin to bombard cells, and a vicious cycle begins anew. A whole host of other effects also come into play as inflammation increases, and triglycerides and blood pressure are raised to mention but a few, to such an extent that we now see a virtual epidemic of what has come to be known as 'metabolic syndrome'. Insulin also blocks your appetite-control hormone leptin so you become more leptin resistant, which makes it even harder to feel satisfied, and this keeps you looking for more energy to take in. Conversely, the release of glucagon, which is the hormone that facilitates the conversion of glycogen in liver cells to glucose, is precipitated by low levels of blood glucose.

In fact, when we lower dietary carbohydrates to 50 grams or less per day, we undergo a process called keto-adaptation. The liver and kidneys begin to metabolise fat for fuel instead, and in the process ketone bodies are formed. Ketone bodies are fragments of fatty acids, which then pass into the bloodstream and from there reach the brain and the rest of the body and replace glucose as an energy source. It takes a little time and consistency in our diet, but after a few weeks of keto-adaptation, more than half the brain's fuel then comes from ketones. The rest indeed comes from glucose, but it seems that this amount can be produced endogenously, via a process called gluconeogenesis during which glucose is made, primarily in the liver, from non-carbohydrate sources.

It must be emphasised though that it is virtually impossible, nor is it advisable, to avoid carb intake entirely – what the low-carb diet suggests is that we take in the minimal amount of glucose so that we maintain our insulin sensitivity, reduce glycation and minimise all the 'diseases of civilisation' associated with high-carb intake, allowing the body to burn fat instead for energy. It is obvious how this use of fat reserves will result in weight loss, which is the main attraction of this diet at present. The sense of satiation is another factor, as fats release energy for a longer period thus diminishing feelings of hunger.

Every randomised controlled trial on low-carb diets has shown that they reduce body fat more than calorie-restricted low-fat diets, lower blood pressure, lower blood sugar and improve symptoms of diabetes, increase HDL (the good) cholesterol, and lower triglycerides and change the pattern of LDL (bad) cholesterol from small, dense (very bad) to large LDL particles.

The 'calories in – calories out' hypothesis

Another long-held belief that has come to be overturned is the one that states essentially that all calories are equal and that there is a dependent relationship between the calories we consume and those we expend. No one can argue that on a simplistic level, the balance between what we consume (calories in) and the energy we expend (calories out) determines whether we sit with a nett gain which will be stored as fat. However, that notion does not take into account the fact that there are several aspects to the 'calories out' side of the equation, including the fact that the body uses energy for day-to-day physiological processes, including the very act of digesting the food that has been taken in, and processing its nutrients and moving them around; and that the energetic 'scales' will also be heavily affected by our levels of physical activity. That said, we also now know that if we restrict calories, the body lowers its resting metabolic rate to help conserve energy, kick-starting a cycle where you have to continuously lower your energy intake to counteract the reduced metabolic rate.

It is now clear that it is not just the *amount* but also the *type* of calories that we eat that affects the equation. Expressed differently, the same number of calories from different types of food can have very different biological effects. Whole foods, for example, take up more metabolic energy to process and digest than processed foods, and protein takes more energy to digest than either fats or carbs. Other factors also come into play, such as the micronutrient factor of a particular calorie source, as well as the potential toxic content by way of the likes of its transfat content, for one.

Another astonishing fact is relevant here – 60% of the caloric intake in the worldwide diet consists of four subsidised, industrialised (and thus mostly GMO) crops: corn, rice, soy and wheat. Where is the diversity in that, where is the micronutrient profile of each of those? Expressed very simply, it's quite obvious that eating 500 calories of French fries or doughnuts would be very different to eating 500 calories of kale chips, the latter being an almost impossible feat anyway. Factor in the fact that foods are now showing lower nutrient levels than they were 50 years ago, a 'calorie is a calorie' becomes even less viable an argument, as what you get out of, say, one serving of broccoli today is not what your Gran did.

Similarly, 'weight loss' is another holy grail of a phrase that is not particularly helpful as it doesn't dig deeper to see if we're losing fat or muscle mass. Have our biomarkers improved in the process or not? This stuff matters if we're pursuing a bigger, longer-term goal of health and wellness.

At the end of the day, let's also never forget that food functions on both a 'hard' biological level and on a 'soft' emotional or psychological one. It certainly is critical to keep our machines running, but food is also a great source of pleasure and comfort, a source of connectedness and a kind of 'glue' that binds families and societies. So rather than obsessing over carb levels in an individual food or meal, might I suggest that you take a longer-term view, placing the bigger picture of health and happiness in front of you as set off down this path?

BASIC BUILDING BLOCKS

SOAKING NUTS AND SEEDS

In the low-carb universe, we use a great deal of nuts and seeds in lieu of grains. However, one of the issues to be aware of when incorporating these in our diet is the level of phytic acid that nuts and seeds contain, as nuts have about the same amount or even higher levels of phytic acid than grains.

Phytic acid is the principal storage form of phosphorus in many plant tissues, especially the bran portion of grains and other seeds. It contains the mineral phosphorus tightly bound in a snowflake-like molecule. In humans and animals with one stomach, the phosphorus is not readily bioavailable. In addition to blocking phosphorus availability, the 'arms' of the phytic acid molecule readily bind with other minerals, such as calcium, magnesium, iron and zinc, making them unavailable as well. Phytic acid not only grabs onto or chelates important minerals, but also inhibits enzymes that we need to digest our food, including pepsin, needed for the breakdown of proteins in the stomach, and amylase, needed for the breakdown of starch into sugar. Trypsin, needed for protein digestion in the small intestine, is also inhibited by phytates.

Phytase is the enzyme that neutralises phytic acid, and co-exists in plant foods that contain phytic acid. In general, though, unlike ruminant animals and even mice, humans do not produce enough phytase to safely consume large quantities of high-phytate foods on a regular basis.

Soaking high phytic acid foods in an acid medium at very warm temperatures, as in the sourdough process, activates phytase and reduces or even eliminates phytic acid. To soak your nuts or seeds, cover them with warm water and let them 'soak' in a warm place for at least 18 hours. I suggest that you drain, rinse and add new water at least once halfway through the process, and throw away the soak water as this now contains some toxins. If you want to be absolutely sure that no bacteria are left behind, you can give them a final rinse with organic apple cider vinegar. After soaking, dehydrate using an oven at a very low temperature, or a food dehydrator or even out in the hot African sun.

Tiny seeds like flax and sesame don't respond that well to soaking, with flax seed becoming a gloopy mess quite quickly. Roasting these is the best possible way to reduce the phytic acid content a little. In general, in fact, if soaking feels like too much hard work, then at the very least roast your nuts and seeds in the oven or in a pan on top of the stove as roasting is also believed to remove a significant portion of phytic acid.

Sprouting also activates phytase, thus reducing phytic acid while increasing the total nutrient density of a food. While you can sprout loads of grains and legumes, the only nuts you can actually sprout successfully are almonds, which will sprout in three days if they're truly raw. Pumpkin and sunflower seeds will also sprout, as will seeds like alfalfa, broccoli, fenugreek and celery. Spread them out on the sprouter stack, giving them a bit of space. Alternatively, use a glass jar, topped with a piece of cheesecloth or muslin held in place with an elastic band. Keep in a dark place and rinse twice a day, tipping the jar upside down to ensure that all the water drains out. A tiny white tail will appear from the narrow end when they begin to sprout. Once you have a decent tail, bring them out into the sunlight for a day so that they can photosynthesise and turn green. Use them right away or store in a jar in the fridge.

Successful sprouting depends on a number of factors including the freshness of the seeds and how 'alive' they are – many nuts and seeds, especially if they have been imported, have been irradiated or chemically treated in some other way, and others are just old. The water's pH, mineral and salt content also affect the process, and sprouting is encouraged in slightly salty and acid water, so you can add a pinch of salt and a spoon of vinegar. After the initial soaking, keep the nuts damp. Put them in a large sieve, and rinse them under the tap a couple of times a day. The nuts need to be kept damp and aired, but not wet, otherwise there is a chance of mould or spoiling.

Probiotic lactobacilli, and other species of the endogenous digestive microflora, can produce phytase so make sure you're taking in enough of this, through incorporating lots of lacto-fermented foods or a good probiotic supplement into your daily regimen.

ALMOND MEAL

Ingredients

Raw almonds, placed in the
freezer for about 6 hours
ahead of making

Instructions

Making your own nut meal is not complicated, but it
does require a food processor. You can work with a
blender, but this will only grind up small amounts at a
time, as would a coffee bean grinder.

Freezing the nuts helps prevent the heating generated
in the grinding process from releasing too much oil too
quickly, and turning your nut meal into nut butter.

The more you grind, the finer the meal that will result,
but take care not to overdo it so that the granules of
nut start to clump up. I find quite a coarse meal more
interesting in terms of giving a more textured end
result, but play around as different levels of granularity
work better in different dishes. Commercially produced
nut meals tend to have a finer, more even consistency,
but it's nice to know you can make your own if you
choose to!

The same really applies with making a meal from any
nut, but take special care with the higher fat nuts as
per the note above.

ALMOND BUTTER

Ingredients

1 kg raw almonds

Approximately 1 cup of oil
(MCT or coconut)

½ teaspoon salt

Instructions

To reduce the phytic acid content, soak your nuts and dehydrate them first.

Place the nuts in the food processor and grind until quite fine. You usually need to stop the processor and use a spatula to prevent the flour clumping in the corners of the bowl. Keeping the blade running, slowly drip in the oil until you get to a consistency that pleases you. Add the salt and blend again thoroughly.

You can also add a little cinnamon or even some chai spices if you'd like to flavour the butter a little differently.

Nut butters make massive overconsumption of what is a high-calorie food group very easy as butter crushes and condenses what's already a dense source of nutrients and energy into a delicious, very more-ish paste. It's VERY hard to stick to just one tablespoon, so avoid nut butters if you can't control yourself around them!

FLAX MEAL

Ingredients
Golden or brown flax seeds

Instructions
As with the nut meals, you can use a food processor or an upright blender or even a coffee grinder to create your own flax meal. As seeds have a lower oil content, you don't need to freeze them before grinding. If you use an upright blender or coffee grinder, work with small amounts at a time or you'll land up with a clumped mess.

Once you've broken the seal so to speak of the seeds by grinding them, you expose more of the surface area to oxidation, so keep the meal in an airtight container in the fridge to prolong shelf life and guard against rancidity.

SUNFLOWER SEED BUTTER

Ingredients

1 kg sunflower seeds, lightly roasted

1 cup oil (coconut, MCT or high oleic)

2–3 tablespoons erythritol/xylitol granules, ground finer in a blender (optional)

Instructions

Place seeds in the food processor and blend until broken down. Add the sweetener if you like and then pulse again.

Slowly drizzle in the oil, to the level of consistency that you prefer.

Store in an airtight jar in the fridge.

As with the almond butter, it's an option to add spices like cinnamon and cardamom to create a specific flavour. Adding some vanilla paste is also a great option.

Nutella Goes A-Banting

Ingredients

180 g roasted hazelnuts

20 g raw cacao or cocoa powder

20 g erythritol/xylitol granules, ground
into a finer form in the blender

40 ml oil (MCT, coconut or high oleic)

Pinch of salt

Instructions

Place the nuts in the food processor and pulse until a meal forms.

Clean out the corners with a spatula and add the cocoa/cacao and the sweetener and pulse again.

With the motor running, slowly add in the oil to the point that you achieve the consistency you like (some of us like it 'runnier' than others).

You can trade out some of the hazels for almonds to lower the cost, but hazelnuts are really the way to go here.

PUMPKIN PIE SPICE

Ingredients

2 tablespoons ground cinnamon
1 teaspoon ground nutmeg
1 teaspoon ground allspice
1 teaspoon ground ginger
½ teaspoon ground cloves
2 pinches of ground cardamom

Instructions

Mix all ingredients thoroughly and store in an airtight container with a secure lid.

Store in a cool, dry place.

If you're able to source fresh (new/freshly ground/unopened) spices, the blend is good for up to a year.

SAVOURY DUKKHA

Ingredients

4 tablespoons cumin seeds
4 tablespoons coriander seeds
1 teaspoon ground cinnamon
1 teaspoon ground nutmeg
1 teaspoon ground cardamom
1 teaspoon ground cloves
2 teaspoons black or yellow
    mustard seeds
1 teaspoon ground fenugreek
¼ cup xylitol syrup
1¾ cups almonds
¼ cup sesame seed

Instructions

Preheat oven to 300°F/150°C. Grease a large baking tray.

Mix the spices into the xylitol syrup and then add the almonds and sesame seed, mixing thoroughly so that the nuts are evenly coated.

Spread the nuts out across the surface of the pan and toast the mixture, raking it over frequently, until the mixture has become dry.

Allow to cool down completely before tipping into the food processor and then blitzing briefly to chop up the nuts and seeds. You can remove some of the mixture and then grind the remainder further so that you have different levels of texture in the dukkha. This adds a wonderful flavour to salads, grilled fish and eggs.

BREAKFAST OPTIONS

BANTING GOJI AND PECAN GRANOLA

Ingredients

100 g pecans
100 g raw almonds
50 g flaked almonds
100 g pumpkin seeds
100 g sunflower seeds
100 g flaked coconut
150 g desiccated coconut
90 ml oil (coconut or MCT)
3 tablespoons erythritol/xylitol
     granules
1 tablespoon ground cinnamon
1 teaspoon ground ginger
½ teaspoon ground nutmeg
1 tablespoon vanilla extract
50 g goji berries

Instructions

Preheat oven to 350°F/180°C.

Mix all the dry ingredients together in a bowl with the exception of the spices.

Warm the oil and the sweetener together over a low heat to dissolve the 'sugar' granules. Add spices to the heated oil – swirl them around, taking care not to burn them.

Allow to cool and add the vanilla extract.

Pour the oil mixture over the nuts and seeds and mix well to make sure the mixture is well coated.

Spoon out onto a baking tray and bake for about 8 minutes, rake through to turn over and then bake for another 8 minutes or until the mixture is toasted and golden brown. Be warned – the coconut catches easily so don't leave it unattended!

Allow to cool, then add the goji berries as these will dry out terribly if you roast them.

Store in an airtight container and use as a breakfast cereal or as a snack.

Double or triple the recipe if you want any meaningful stash to remain in the pantry after you've tasted it the first time.

BASIC SWEET MUFFIN MIXTURE

Makes 6 large or 12 small muffins

Ingredients

Filling

Grated apple, fresh or frozen
   berries, dried cranberries,
   chopped nuts and seeds, etc.

Muffins

1 cup coconut flour
½ cup almond meal
½ cup flax meal
¼ cup erythritol/xylitol granules
½ teaspoon salt
1 teaspoon baking powder
½ teaspoon baking soda
3 free-range or pastured eggs
1 cup buttermilk
1 teaspoon vanilla extract
¼ cup oil (coconut or MCT)
½ cup coconut milk
¼ cup water

Instructions

Preheat oven to 350°F/180°C. Line a muffin pan with paper baking cups or butter well to prevent sticking.

Prepare your filling – fresh strawberries are great, as are frozen cranberries and toasted chopped nuts and seeds. Lemon zest is always a great addition.

Mix the dry ingredients well together. Then beat the eggs and blend these with the remaining wet ingredients. Add the wet to the dry and stir through well to combine, ensuring there are no lumps.

Then add the filling ingredients. Spoon into the muffin cups and add a topping if you like – some more chopped nuts, desiccated coconut, citrus zest, poppy seeds, etc.

Bake for 30–40 minutes or until toothpick inserted comes out clean. Allow to cool a little before serving with loads of butter.

GOJI BERRY, ORANGE AND PECAN MUFFINS

Makes 6 large or 12 small muffins

Ingredients

6 free-range or pastured eggs

½ cup melted butter or coconut oil
  or MCT oil

1 teaspoon pure vanilla extract

¼ cup xylitol syrup

Zest and juice of 1 orange

½ cup coconut flour

½ teaspoon salt

¼ teaspoon baking soda

½ cup chopped pecans

½ cup goji berries

Extra pecans and orange zest for
  topping

Instructions

Preheat oven to 350°F/180°C. Grease muffin cups or line with paper cups and spray with non-stick spray.

Whisk the eggs, butter or oil, vanilla, syrup, orange zest and juice together in a large bowl.

Sift the coconut flour, salt and baking soda, add to the wet ingredients and stir until well combined. Carefully fold in the pecans and goji berries.

Fill muffin cups to ¾ full with batter. If you like, sprinkle a few extra pecans and a little extra orange zest on the top of each muffin to create a nice surface and for extra nuttiness.

Bake for 35–40 minutes for large muffins and about 20–25 minutes for smaller ones.

These store well as they are very moist. If kept in an airtight container in the fridge, they should last for at least 5 days.

SOUR CREAM BLUEBERRY MUFFINS

Makes 6 muffins

Ingredients

1½ cups almond meal
½ cup flax meal
¼ cup erythritol/xylitol granules
½ teaspoon baking soda
¼ teaspoon salt
½ teaspoon ground cinnamon
2 free-range or pastured eggs
1 cup sour cream
2 tablespoons melted butter
150 g fresh or frozen blueberries
Flaked almonds or coconut flakes
    for topping

Instructions

Preheat oven to 350°F/180°C. Line a muffin pan with cupcake papers and grease well.

Whisk together almond meal and other dry ingredients.

In a separate bowl, lightly beat the eggs, and then mix in the sour cream and butter until smooth.

Add the sour cream mixture to the almond meal mixture and stir until mixed well.

Add blueberries and stir until evenly distributed.

Spoon mixture into the muffin cups, filling each cupcake paper about ¾ full. Sprinkle over some flaked almonds or coconut flakes to create a nice crunchy topping.

Bake for about 20 minutes or until golden. Allow to cool a little before serving.

These are wonderfully moist, courtesy of the sour cream, and will keep well in the fridge.

PUMPKIN AND CREAM CHEESE MUFFINS

Makes 12 small muffins

Ingredients

Candied pumpkin seeds

½ tablespoon butter

¼ cup pumpkin seeds

1 tablespoon erythritol/xylitol
    granules

¼ teaspoon ground cinnamon

Cream cheese filling

240 g cream cheese, softened

2 tablespoons cream

2 teaspoons vanilla extract

Muffins

¾ cup pumpkin purée

1¼ cups almond meal

1¼ cups coconut flour

½ cup flax meal

⅓ cup unflavoured pure whey
    isolate protein powder

2 teaspoons baking powder

½ teaspoon baking soda

½ teaspoon salt

1½ teaspoon ground cinnamon

½ teaspoon ground ginger

¼ teaspoon ground cloves

¼ cup butter, softened

½ cup erythritol/xylitol granules

3 large free-range or pastured eggs

1 teaspoon vanilla extract

¼ cup unsweetened coconut milk

Instructions

Preheat oven to 350°F/180°C. Line 12 muffin tins with paper liners, greasing these well.

To make the pumpkin purée, steam about 500 g of cubed pumpkin until soft. Allow to drain and then blend in a food processor or with a hand-beater/stick-blender. If it is very wet, then reduce it slightly in a pot.

For the candied pumpkin seeds, melt the butter in a small skillet over medium heat. Add seeds and toss to coat. Add sweetener and cinnamon and toss to coat. Remove from heat and set aside.

For the cream cheese filling, beat cream cheese with the cream and vanilla extract until smooth. Set aside.

For the muffins, in a medium bowl, whisk together the almond meal and coconut flour, flax meal, protein powder, baking powder, baking soda, salt and spices.

In a large bowl, beat butter with sweetener until well combined. Beat in pumpkin purée, eggs and vanilla extract.

Beat in almond meal mixture in two additions, alternating with coconut milk.

Drop a spoonful of batter into the bottom of prepared muffin tins and use a spoon to make a well in the centre. Drop a tablespoon of cream cheese filling into the well, then top with more batter to fill muffin tins to about ¾ full.

Sprinkle each muffin with some candied pumpkin seeds.

Bake for 23–25 minutes, or until tops are set and edges are just browned. Allow to cool in pan for 15 minutes before transferring to a wire rack to cool completely.

BERRY BLINTZES WITH CREAM CHEESE

Makes 4 crêpes or 2 portions

Ingredients

Filling

100 g chunky cottage cheese
100 g cream cheese
1 teaspoon vanilla extract
2 teaspoons erythritol/xylitol
    granules

Berry compote

250 g mixed fresh or frozen berries,
    defrosted
50 ml water
1 tablespoon erythritol/xylitol
    granules

Crêpes

2 free-range or pastured eggs
2 tablespoons oil (coconut or MCT)
    or butter, melted, plus more for
    frying
1 teaspoon erythritol/xylitol
    granules
⅛ teaspoon salt
2 tablespoons sifted coconut flour
⅓ cup whole milk

Instructions

For the filling, mix the ingredients well together so that the elements are completely integrated. Depending on the thickness of cream cheese, you may need to 'loosen' the mixture with a drop of milk or water. Set aside. Xylitol syrup will blend in without any granularity, but if you don't have this, then you can put the sweetener in your blender to create a finer powder.

For the berry compote, place all ingredients in a pan and simmer gently until the fruit has softened and the sweetener is totally dissolved and has become syrupy. Set aside.

For the crêpes, blend together the eggs, oil or butter, sweetener and salt.

Thoroughly mix in coconut flour. Stir in milk.

Heat 1 tablespoon of coconut oil in a small skillet. Pour a quarter of the batter into the skillet; immediately rotate it until a thin even layer of batter covers the bottom of the skillet. The crêpe should be about 15 cm in diameter.

Cook until batter is bubbly and cooked around the edges. Turn and cook other side. Repeat with the balance of the crêpe mixture, storing the prepared crêpes on a plate.

To serve, place a few tablespoons of the cream cheese mixture in the centre of each crêpe. Fold in the 'sides' and then roll up into a log.

Lie one crêpe at right angles over the other and then spoon over the warmed berry compote. Garnish with extra fresh berries if you have some!

BLUEBERRY FRITTATA

Serves 4–6

Ingredients

6 free-range or pastured eggs
1½ cups milk of choice, such as full-
    cream dairy or coconut milk
½ cup coconut flour
1 teaspoon vanilla extract
1 teaspoon ground cinnamon
½ teaspoon salt
1 tablespoon coconut oil
200 g fresh or frozen blueberries
    (defrosted and drained)
Mascarpone to serve

Instructions

Preheat oven to 425°F/220°C.

Combine eggs, milk, flour, vanilla, cinnamon and salt. Whisk briskly until smooth.

Place oil in cast-iron frying pan and swish it around to coat up the sides of the pan.

Pour batter into the pan and then sprinkle over the blueberries. You could use fresh strawberries, chunks of apple or a mixture of frozen berries (defrosted and drained so you remove the water).

Cook for a few minutes over a medium flame and then place pan in the oven and bake for 15–20 minutes or until the egg has set nicely.

Remove from oven and serve with a dollop of mascarpone as a delightful weekend breakfast treat!

BREAKFAST IN A BAR

Makes 8 bars

Ingredients

¼ cup goji berries or
    hazelnuts, chopped
120 g almond meal
70 g coconut flour
¼ teaspoon salt
¼ teaspoon baking soda
¼ cup coconut or MCT oil
¼ cup xylitol syrup
1 free-range or pastured egg
1 teaspoon vanilla extract
½ cup unsweetened
    desiccated coconut
½ cup pumpkin seeds
½ cup sunflower seeds

Instructions

Preheat oven to 350°F/180°C. Grease a 20x20-cm baking dish with coconut oil or butter.

If using goji berries, pour warm water over to plump them up and provide extra moisture so they don't dry out too much while baking.

In a small bowl, combine almond meal, coconut flour, salt and baking soda.

In a large bowl, combine oil, xylitol syrup, egg and vanilla, and then stir dry ingredients into wet.

Mix in coconut, pumpkin seeds, sunflower seeds and gojis/hazelnuts.

Press the dough into the baking dish, wetting your hands with water if needs be to help pat the dough down evenly.

Bake for 20 minutes. Cool bars in pan, then slice and serve or store in an airtight container.

CHEESY SAVOURY MUFFINS

Makes 6 muffins

Ingredients

Muffins

270 g chunky cottage cheese or
    ricotta
80 g Parmesan, grated
4 large free-range or pastured eggs
¾ cup water
40 g tapioca flour
110 g coconut flour
40 g almond meal
1 teaspoon baking powder
½ teaspoon smoked paprika
¼ teaspoon salt
Black pepper

Filling

Roasted peppers, caramelised
    tomatoes, grilled zucchini (baby
    marrows), wilted Swiss chard
    or spinach, crispy bacon bits,
    smoked chicken strips, cubed
    smoked salmon or salmon trout,
    prosciutto, fresh herbs, etc!

Instructions

Preheat oven to 350°F/180°C. Line a muffin pan with paper baking cups and spray them lightly with non-stick spray or simply grease pan well.

Whisk the cottage cheese, Parmesan, eggs and water together in a large bowl.

Add the tapioca and coconut flour, almond meal, baking powder, smoked paprika and salt, and whisk until no lumps remain.

Fold in the filling ingredients, turning through well to distribute the filling evenly. I like more filling and less batter, but you can dial that up or down according to your own preferences.

Divide the mixture between the muffin cups, grind over some black pepper or sprinkle some paprika and freshly chopped herbs over the tops. Bake for 30–35 minutes until puffed and golden brown.

These store well in the fridge, but they are best warmed slightly before serving so that the cheeses soften a little.

ENGLISH MUFFINS

Makes 6 muffins

Ingredients

½ cup almond meal
½ cup coconut flour
4 tablespoons flax meal
2 teaspoons psyllium husk powder
1 teaspoon baking soda
1 teaspoon baking powder
½ teaspoon salt
4 free-range or pastured eggs, beaten
2 tablespoons oil (coconut or MCT)
120 ml filtered water
A grinding of black pepper, pinch
   of paprika and pinch of mustard
   powder

Instructions

Preheat oven to 350°F/180°C (if baking the muffins).

Whisk together the dry ingredients in a small bowl.

Add the remaining wet ingredients and stir through well until fully incorporated.

Transfer the mixture into greased microwave-safe ramekins or into flat English muffin pans if you're going to bake them in the oven.

Microwave for 2 minutes or bake for approximately 12 minutes. Allow to cool slightly, then remove from the ramekin/pan and slice the muffins in half. I have to confess that I think they come out better in the microwave!

You can then toast them in a toaster if you like or under a grill for a few minutes to crisp up the surface.

These freeze well so you can bake a batch and then defrost overnight. Alternatively, the mixture will keep in the fridge for at least 4 days, allowing you to bake them daily if you prefer.

They're great served with poached eggs, some wilted Swiss chard, smoked salmon, salmon trout or crispy bacon if you prefer.

SALMON AND EGG POTS

Serves 6

Ingredients

7 free-range or pastured eggs
1 cup spinach, Swiss chard or kale, chopped
1 cup cherry/Rosa tomatoes, halved
6 slices smoked salmon/salmon trout
¼ cup feta cheese, crumbled
¼ cup almond meal
½ teaspoon finely chopped garlic
A few basil leaves, snipped into fine strips
1 teaspoon salt
Grinding of black pepper
Pinch of cayenne pepper
Flat-leaf parsley or coriander, chopped

Instructions

Preheat oven to 350°F/180°C. Grease large muffin tins or small ramekins.

In a medium-sized bowl, crack open the eggs and mix well with a fork or whisk. Add in the rest of the ingredients and mix well. Feel free to use up leftover bits of grilled salmon, bacon or mince in place of the salmon trout.

Spoon mixture into the individual containers and top with a sprinkling of parsley or coriander.

Bake for 20 minutes, until the middle of the muffin is firm to the touch.

These will store refrigerated in an airtight container for up to 5 days.

BREAKFAST PIZZAS

Makes 2 pizzas

Ingredients

Crust

2–3 medium sweet potatoes
(enough to yield 1 cup of mash)
1 cup almond meal
1 teaspoon baking soda
1 tablespoon Italian seasoning
1 teaspoon salt

Topping

1 tablespoon coconut oil
4 free-range or pastured eggs,
fried
200 g bacon or pancetta, pan-fried
(or ham, smoked salmon, etc.)
1 handful of kale, spinach or baby
spinach leaves or even rocket
1 tablespoon fresh basil/flat-leaf
parsley or both
½ cup mozzarella cheese (optional)
Rosa tomatoes (halved)
Olive oil to drizzle
Salt and black pepper

Instructions

Preheat oven to 350°F/180°C.

Set a large pot of water to boil. Peel and cut your sweet potatoes into cubes. Add potatoes to boiling water, turn down to simmer, and boil them for about 20 minutes or until a knife easily pierces the flesh. Drain potatoes from the water and mash well in a large bowl. Instead of boiling you can also roast them, which I think is nicer and preserves the mineral content better.

Add 1 cup of your sweet potato mash, almond meal, baking soda and seasoning to a large bowl. Knead well together with your hands until the mixture resembles a ball of pizza dough.

Line a baking tray or pizza pan with parchment paper, and press out the dough to a large circle. The dough should be about 5–7 mm thick.

Bake in the oven for 15–20 minutes or until the edges of the dough are slightly browned.

While the pizza is in the oven, pan-fry the eggs in oil and slice up the other topping ingredients. You really can top this with whatever makes for a breakfast pizza, as opposed to an 'any other time' kind of pizza!

Remove your pizza from the oven, add your preferred toppings, including the eggs, and then pop under the grill for 3–5 minutes until cheese is melted.

Top with fresh greens and chopped herbs and serve.

SWEET POTATO CUPS

Makes 12 small cups

Ingredients

Potato cups

1 tablespoon coconut oil, MCT oil
   or melted butter or ghee
1 medium onion, sliced into thin
   strips
2 sweet potatoes, peeled and
   grated
1 tablespoon coconut flour
2 large free-range or pastured eggs
1 teaspoon salt
Ground black pepper to taste

Filling

Any kind of leftover curry or
   casserole is great here, as is
   leftover mince, spiked with a bit
   of chilli. Roasted veggies are
   another nice option and you
   can also fill them with whisked
   eggs and some chopped bacon,
   sliced chorizo or salmon strips,
   herbs and some wilted greens.

Instructions

Preheat oven to 350°F/180°C. Grease a muffin pan or silicon baking cups.

Melt the oil or butter over a fairly high heat. Add in the onion and cook until it caramelises. Set aside.

Grate the sweet potatoes. This is where a food processor is really helpful. Pat the grated mixture dry with a paper towel to remove as much moisture as you can. Put the grated potatoes, cooked onions and the rest of your ingredients together in a bowl and mix well.

Spoon mixture into each cup. Then use your fingers, a spoon or even the pestle part of a mortar-and-pestle to press down the mixture evenly along the base and up the sides of the cups so that a little basket is created.

Bake for 25 minutes or so until they feel dry enough to handle.

Remove from oven and allow to cool slightly, then turn the cups upside down onto a flat baking tray. Return tray to the oven and crisp up for an additional 10 minutes upside down. Handle carefully so that you maintain the structure of your cups.

Add your filling into the cups and then bake again for about 15 minutes until the filling has 'set'. You could also scramble the eggs first and then pile this mixture into the cups with crispy bacon bits and some caramelised Rosa tomatoes, for example. Very nice served with a little rocket on the side to break the richness of the eggs!

CRUSTLESS FOUR-CHEESE BRUNCH QUICHE

Makes 1 quiche

Ingredients

10 free-range or pastured eggs
Grinding of black pepper
Pinch of paprika
Pinch of mustard powder
1 teaspoon salt
⅔ cup buttermilk, yoghurt or
    coconut cream
225 g Swiss chard or spinach, wilted
200 g Rosa tomatoes, halved
80 g chorizo, sliced thinly
60 g cheddar, shredded
40 g pecorino, grated
70 g gorgonzola, crumbled
75 g goat's milk or crumbly Greek-
    style feta, cubed or crumbled
2 teaspoons garlic chives, chopped

Instructions

Preheat oven to 350°F/180°C. Grease a quiche, pie
dish or springform pan.

Whisk the eggs, spices and liquid of choice until
smooth. Mix in the wilted greens, tomatoes, chorizo
and half the cheese.

Pour into quiche or pie dish. Top with the remaining
cheese and garlic chives.

Bake for 40 minutes or until set in the centre.

Feel free to trade out the veg and chorizo for other
options such as roasted peppers, shredded, smoked
or roast chicken, etc.

Zucchini, Cashew and Mushroom Loaf

Serves 12

Ingredients

1½ cups cashews or mixed cashews, hazels and almonds

4 medium zucchini (baby marrows), grated

1 tablespoon oil (coconut or MCT)

1 onion, chopped (red onion is always nice)

1 clove garlic, finely chopped

200 g button mushrooms

4 free-range or pastured eggs

Salt and black pepper

Pinch of paprika

¼ cup almond meal

1 cup grated cheddar cheese

Sprig of thyme or marjoram for topping

Instructions

Preheat oven to 350°F/180°C. Grease a loaf tin well.

Process the nuts roughly until they're in smallish pieces so that they still have some substance.

Grate the zucchini and allow to stand in a colander so that the moisture released from cutting drains off. Pat with a tea towel or paper towel to remove any remaining moisture.

Pan-fry the onion and garlic in the coconut oil until soft, then add the mushrooms, cooking until these are soft and all moisture has been absorbed.

In a mixing bowl, beat the eggs lightly and add the spices. Add the almond meal, nuts and cheese to the onion and mushroom mixture and then add the grated zucchini. Freshly chopped Swiss chard, kale or spinach make great alternatives to the zucchini. Add the beaten egg mixture to the vegetable mixture and stir through thoroughly.

Spoon mixture into the tin and bake for an hour or until the loaf feels firm to the touch. This is a great weekend brunch dish, served with rocket and caramelised Rosa tomatoes as the sharpness of these two contrasts nicely with the richness of the egg and almond combo.

Garnish with thyme or marjoram before serving.

SNACKS AND NIBBLES

PARMESAN AND POPPY SEED LOLLIES

Makes 20–24 lollies

Ingredients

160 g Parmesan, finely grated
2 tablespoons poppy seeds
2 tablespoons sesame seeds

Instructions

Preheat oven to 425°F/220°C. Line two large baking trays with greased baking paper.

Toss the cheese and seeds together in a small bowl. Place a 6-cm ring or cookie cutter on one of the baking trays and sprinkle a small handful of the cheese mixture into it, in a thin layer.

Carefully lift the ring off to reveal a neat-edged disc of Parmesan and lay a lollipop stick on top, with the tip of the stick touching the middle of the disc. Repeat with the remaining cheese and sticks (leaving about 3-cm spaces between them to allow for any spreading during cooking).

You should have a little cheese left over, so use it to cover up the part of the lollipop stick resting on the disc. Bake in the oven for 5 minutes. The cheese should be lightly golden and bubbling. Remove from the oven and slide the paper off the baking trays and onto a rack to help speed up cooling.

Leave to cool for 1–2 minutes until the lollipops have become crisp. Very carefully remove each one with a palette knife. Big people and little people love these and they're fun for parties.

SWEET CHILLI CASHEWS

Ingredients

1 teaspoon cayenne pepper or
  chilli powder
1 teaspoon curry powder (medium
  to hot depending on your
  capacity for heat)
½ teaspoon salt
3 tablespoons xylitol syrup
2 cups cashews (or any nut you
  prefer – macs are also great in
  this recipe)

Instructions

Preheat oven to 300°F/150°C. Grease a baking tray.

Blend the spices with the xylitol syrup and add a little water if you feel you need to loosen it up a bit. Pour over the nuts and mix really well, so that each nut is evenly coated.

Spoon onto the tray and distribute evenly across the surface. Place in the oven and roast for about 10 minutes.

Remove tray and rake nuts before returning to oven to roast for another 5–8 minutes or until the wet mixture has dried off and the nuts are golden. Allow to cool completely before storing.

SPICY SEED MIX

Ingredients

60 ml olive oil
5 red chillies, seeds removed
1 teaspoon garlic, crushed or finely
    chopped
2 red peppers (about 700 g)
3 beef tomatoes (about 400 g),
    blanched, skinned and cut into
    wedges
1 teaspoon ground fenugreek
A handful each of fresh mint and
    coriander
2 teaspoons lemon juice
1 teaspoon white wine vinegar
Salt and black pepper to taste
800 g pumpkin seeds
800 g sunflower seeds

Instructions

Preheat oven to 375°F/190°C.

Grease a roasting pan with a little of the olive oil. Roast the chilli, garlic, peppers and tomatoes together, spooning them around now and then to make sure they are coated with the oil, and roast for about 30 minutes until soft.

Remove the tray from the oven and place the peppers in a bowl, covering with plastic wrap for 15 minutes so that they steam a little, which will help you to remove the skins.

Place everything in a blender, adding the fenugreek, balance of the oil and the herbs and blend until smooth. Season to taste and then add the lemon juice, vinegar and salt. Blend again.

Place the seeds in a large bowl and then pour over the spicy sauce, mixing through with your hands to make sure each seed gets a good dose of sauce.

Spread out seed mixture onto several baking trays, and roast for about 30 minutes, raking through every now and then, until the sauce has 'dried up' and the seeds have turned golden brown.

Allow to cool completely before storing in an airtight container. This mixture is great as a snack or sprinkled over salads.

North African Spicy Almonds

Ingredients

2 tablespoons olive oil
½ teaspoon ground cumin
½ teaspoon chilli powder
½ teaspoon curry powder
½ teaspoon garlic salt
¼ teaspoon cayenne pepper
¼ teaspoon powdered ginger
¼ teaspoon ground cinnamon
2 cups whole almonds, shelled
1½ teaspoons salt

Instructions

Preheat oven to 300°F/150°C. Grease a flat baking tray.

In a non-stick skillet heat the olive oil and spices over a low heat for 3 or so minutes.

Place the nuts in a bowl and pour oil mixture over the top, toss and stir well to coat each nut with the oil mixture.

Then, spread nuts into a single layer on the baking tray and pop into the oven for 15 minutes, shaking the tray about every 5 minutes or so to cook evenly.

Remove from oven and sprinkle with salt. Let cool for two hours. Store in an airtight container.

NACHOS/TORTILLA CHIPS

Ingredients

⅓ cup + 1 tablespoon flax meal
1½ tablespoons coconut flour
½ cup almond meal
1 tablespoon psyllium husk powder
½ teaspoon salt
Grinding of black pepper
Pinch of chilli powder
Handful of fresh coriander,
    chopped
1 tablespoon chia meal
½ cup water, lukewarm (+ 1–2
    tablespoons if the dough still
    feels too dry)
2 tablespoons melted ghee, butter
    or coconut oil for brushing
Guacamole/tzatziki/sour cream dip/
    tomato, red onion and coriander
    salsa, etc. to serve

Instructions

Preheat the oven to 400°F/200°C. Grease a baking tray.

Place the flax meal, coconut flour, almond meal and psyllium husk powder into a bowl.

Add the seasoning, coriander and then the chia meal.

Pour in the water and then combine well using your hands. If needed, add a few more tablespoons of water. However, if you use too much, the dough will get too sticky and difficult to roll. Let the dough rest in the fridge or on the kitchen counter for up to an hour.

Roll out the dough to a thickness of about 4 mm. Use a small 10-cm diameter lid or bowl to cut out a round shape. Repeat for the remaining of the dough.

Use a pizza cutter or a sharp knife to cut the rounds into 6 equal triangles. Place the triangles (tortilla chips) on the greased baking tray.

Melt the ghee (or butter or coconut oil) and brush onto each of the tortilla chips. Place in the oven and bake until lightly browned and crispy. This could take 10–15 minutes. If the tortilla chips don't bake evenly, remove piecemeal from the oven to prevent those that are ready from getting burnt.

Allow to cool before serving with a variety of dips, and a shot of tequila (the latter being optional).

CHILLI SWEET POTATO CHIPS

Serves 3–4

Ingredients

2 organic sweet potatoes
2 tablespoons macadamia oil
2 teaspoons fine chilli powder
½ teaspoon garlic powder or
    1 teaspoon finely minced
    fresh garlic
½ teaspoon salt
Black pepper, to taste
Homemade mayo, aioli or tzatziki
    to dip

Instructions

Preheat oven to 300°F/120°C. Grease 2 baking trays.

Scrub the outside of the sweet potatoes until very clean. The skin will be left on, so try to find organic pesticide-free sweet potatoes. Pat dry.

Cut off both ends of the sweet potato. Use a mandolin or a very sharp knife to slice the sweet potato into 3–4-mm thin medallions (a mandolin works best for perfect even circles, which helps with the baking process. Your chips will be less likely to have chewy spots then).

Mix the spices into the macadamia oil. Throw the potato slices into a large mixing bowl and then pour over the macadamia nut oil mixture, mixing thoroughly until all slices are evenly coated with spice.

Lay out the slices in a single layer on the two baking trays.

Bake for about an hour (depending on chip thickness), pulling the trays out periodically to flip the chips and rotate the baking trays if needs be. This will help with even baking. It's best to keep a watchful eye towards the end since they can burn quickly, especially if they're quite thin.

Serve with a dip of your choice. These chips are best eaten the day they are made, though you can crisp up again by popping into a low oven for a few minutes. There are unlikely to be any left over though!

CHILLI, MAC AND COCO MIX

Ingredients

30 ml organic coconut oil
3–4 fresh red chillies, seeds
    removed
1 teaspoon ground paprika
50 g erythritol/xylitol granules
    (preferably ground to a finer
    consistency in a blender)
500 g macadamias, whole or in
    pieces
250 g flaked coconut
Salt and black pepper to taste

Instructions

Preheat oven to 325°F/160°C. Grease two baking trays with a little coconut oil.

Slice chillies into fine 1–2-mm rings. Place paprika, chilli, sweetener and remaining coconut oil in a saucepan and heat through so that the sweetener melts into the oil. You could also use xylitol syrup here, obviously. Allow to cool.

Place the macs and coconut in a large mixing bowl, and pour over the spice mixture. Mix thoroughly to ensure that each nut and flake is evenly coated. Season with salt and black pepper.

Spread mixture out onto baking trays and roast the mixture in the oven for about 20 minutes, raking it over every now and then to ensure even browning. Watch the coconut as it turns before the nuts. Allow to cool completely. Adjust saltiness if you like and store in an airtight container.

SAVOURY CRACKERS

HERB AND CHILLI CRACKERS

Makes 24 crackers

Ingredients

1 cup sunflower seeds

1 cup sesame seeds

2 teaspoons mixed dried herbs or freshly chopped organic basil, thyme and/or oregano

¼–½ teaspoon dried fine chilli

½ teaspoon finely chopped fresh garlic

Pinch of salt and grinding of black pepper

⅓ cup water (approximately)

1 tablespoon olive oil

Instructions

Preheat oven to 350°F/180°C. Grease a baking tray with coconut oil or butter.

In a food processor, create a meal from the sunflower seeds (it will take about 2–3 minutes for the seeds to break down and turn into a more flour-like consistency, although it will be thicker and heavier than regular flour).

Add the sesame seeds, herbs and seasoning and pulse a few times (or mix in by hand). Slowly add water first and then the olive oil, stirring or pulsing until a thick paste forms that can be rolled out.

Press the mixture into the baking tray, so that it is evenly spread across the entire surface. Lightly score the surface of the mixture into 24 squares with a sharp knife, and sprinkle with some additional dried herbs if you'd like.

Bake until golden and crisp, for about 20 minutes. Allow to cool thoroughly before removing from the tin and then gently breaking into squares as scored. Store in an airtight container.

ALMOND AND PARMESAN CRACKERS

Makes 24 crackers

Ingredients

225 g almond meal

¾ teaspoon baking soda

1 clove garlic, minced

2 tablespoon finely chopped fresh
    or dried basil or thyme

110 g Parmesan, finely grated

2 tablespoons olive oil

1 teaspoon salt

Grinding of black pepper

3–4 tablespoons water

Instructions

Preheat oven to 350°F/180°C. Grease a baking tray with butter or coconut oil.

In a mixing bowl or food processor, combine all ingredients and stir to form a moist, sticky dough. Add more water or oil if needed.

Using dampened hands, press the dough into the baking tray and, using your fingers, flatten the dough out into a uniform thin layer free of cracks. Score the surface of the dough to mark out 24 crackers.

Bake for 15 minutes or until dough becomes dry and golden in appearance.

Remove and cool on a wire rack. Once the crackers have cooled slightly (and this is important, because they become very brittle right out of the oven), use a pizza cutter or sharp knife to draw along the lines created earlier to separate the crackers. Store in an airtight container.

MIXED SEED AND NUT CRACKERS

Makes 24 crackers

Ingredients
½ cup almond meal
½ cup macadamia nuts
1 tablespoon coconut flour
¼ cup pumpkin seeds
2 tablespoons sunflower seeds
2 tablespoons sesame seeds
2 tablespoons hemp seeds
1 tablespoon flax meal
½ teaspoon salt
Grinding of black pepper
1 tablespoon butter, melted
¼ cup water

Instructions
Preheat oven to 350°F/180°C. Grease a baking tray with coconut oil or butter.

Pulse almond meal, macadamias and coconut flour in a food processor until well blended.

Pulse in the seeds, flax meal and seasoning until almost fully ground, leaving a little chunkiness for texture.

Pulse in the melted butter, then the water. The dough will form a ball in the food processor.

Roll out the dough between 2 pieces of parchment paper to about 3–4 mm thick and then cut out shapes, transferring them to the baking tray. Alternatively, press the dough directly into the tray, and then score the sheet of dough into rectangular shapes. Makes about 24 crackers if you score 4 along the short side and 6 along the long side of the tin.

Bake for 20–25 minutes.

Allow to cool before cutting along the score marks to separate the crackers. Store in an airtight container.

Sunflower, Sesame and Almond Crackers

Makes approximately 24 crackers

Ingredients

130 g sunflower seeds

90 g almond meal

1 teaspoon psyllium husk

1 teaspoon baking powder

2 tablespoons full-cream organic
    milk

1 free-range or pastured egg

25 g salted butter, melted

25 g sesame seeds

Instructions

Preheat oven to 350°F/180°C. Grease a baking tray.

Grind the sunflower seeds into a rough meal and then mix this with the almond meal, psyllium husk and baking powder in a bowl.

Blend together the milk and egg and stir into the ground seed and almond mixture with the melted butter, mixing well. Gently work the mixture with your hands to form a moist dough.

Roll out the dough to 3.5 mm thickness on a cool surface, lightly dusted with a little extra almond meal to prevent sticking. Sprinkle the sesame seeds across the surface of the dough, pressing down with the palm of your hand and cut into shapes, transferring to the baking tray. Alternatively press the dough directly into the baking tray, spreading it out as evenly as possible, and scoring the dough lightly to demarcate the crackers.

Bake for about 10 minutes, until lightly browned. Remove from the oven and leave for a minute or two. Transfer to a wire rack and leave to cool.

ROSEMARY AND GARLIC CRACKERS

Makes approximately 40 crackers

Ingredients

450 g almond meal
150 g coconut flour
1 teaspoon finely chopped garlic
1 teaspoon salt
1 teaspoon chopped, fresh or dried
    rosemary
2 large free-range or pastured eggs
2 tablespoons melted butter or
    olive oil

Instructions

Preheat oven to 350°F/180°C. Grease 2 standard baking trays well.

In a medium-sized bowl stir together the almond meal and coconut flour, garlic, salt and rosemary.

In a small bowl beat eggs. Whisk in butter or olive oil. Mix well.

Pour wet ingredients into dry. Mix well with a fork and then knead a few times in the bowl until dough comes together well. Form the dough into a ball.

Divide the dough, placing half into the centre of each of the baking trays. Using your fingers and knuckles, press the dough across the surface of the tray, working from the centre out. Keep working to spread the dough as thin and evenly as possible. Flatten uneven bits with the palm of your hand and finally use the back of a spoon to smooth the surface one final time.

Use a sharp knife to cut the dough into evenly sized squares. Then use a fork to poke each cracker twice.

Bake for 11–15 minutes or until golden brown around the edges. Place on a wire rack and separate crackers once cooled.

If your dough wasn't perfectly even and thin enough, remove the thinner, crisper crackers and place the balance of the crackers back in the oven for an additional 5 minutes or until crisp and firm.

Store in an airtight container.

COCONUT AND CHEDDAR CRACKERS

Makes 24 crackers

Ingredients

½ cup almond meal

2 free-range or pastured eggs

¼ cup butter, melted

¼ teaspoon salt

3 cups mature cheddar cheese,
    shredded

½ cup sifted coconut flour

Instructions

Preheat oven to 350°F/180°C. Grease a baking tray.

Blend together almond meal, eggs, butter, salt and cheese.

Add coconut flour and knead the dough with your hands for 2–3 minutes.

Press the dough into the baking tray so that it lies evenly across the surface (alternatively form the dough into 2.5-cm diameter balls, place on the baking tray and flatten to a diameter of about 5 cm and then use a cookie cutter if you prefer a round shape).

Bake for 15 minutes.

Allow to cool slightly, then slice into 24 squares (or fewer larger ones if you prefer). Store in an airtight container, but be aware that these don't last for very long given the high percentage of cheese they contain. You can crisp up the crackers by reheating at a slightly higher temperature than you baked them for about 4 minutes.

Feel free to add a bit of ground chilli or paprika to introduce a slightly more piquant flavour.

BREADS, WRAPS AND PIZZAS

SEEDED BURGER BUNS

Makes 4 buns

Ingredients

2 free-range or pastured egg whites
2 whole free-range or pastured
    eggs
1 cup mixed seeds (pumpkin,
    sunflower, flax and sesame)
4 tablespoons almond meal
4 tablespoons psyllium husk
1 teaspoon baking powder
Pinch of salt
Little olive oil (approximately 30 ml)

Instructions

Preheat oven to 350°F/180°C. Grease a large muffin tin or English muffin pan well.

Beat the 2 egg whites until frothy.

Mix all other ingredients together well and then fold in the whipped egg whites.

Divide the mixture into four muffin or English muffin portions.

Bake for 30 minutes and allow to cool before removing from tin.

Make sure your burger patties are made from free-range, grass-fed meat. A flattened, free-range chicken breast is another nice option, as is a piece of grilled salmon.

Garnish your burgers with loads of rocket, a herbed mayo and even some pickles if you enjoy these.

PUMPKIN BAGELS

Makes 6 medium or 12 mini bagels

Ingredients

⅓ cup coconut flour, sifted

3 tablespoons flax meal

1 tablespoon psyllium husk

½ teaspoon xanthan gum

¼ teaspoon salt

3 free-range or pastured eggs, beaten

½ cup pumpkin purée

1 teaspoon pumpkin pie spice blend

¼ cup coconut or full-cream diary milk

2 tablespoons butter or coconut oil, melted

½ teaspoon baking soda

1 teaspoon apple cider vinegar

Instructions

Preheat oven to 350°F/180°C. Grease or oil a bagel or doughnut pan really well (mini versions are great for a weekend brunch or even as a canapé).

In a large mixing bowl combine sifted coconut flour, flax meal, psyllium, xanthan and salt. Mix together well. Set aside.

In a separate mixing bowl combine eggs, pumpkin purée (see page 34 for recipe), pumpkin spice, milk of choice and melted butter or coconut oil.

Mix baking soda and apple cider vinegar together in a small bowl and then add this to egg mixture and stir together.

Add this mixture to coconut flour mixture. Stir thoroughly until batter is smooth.

Spoon the mixture into pan forms and spread around with the back of a spoon or a spatula. Wipe the edges of the centre hole area clean with damp paper towel.

Bake for 20–25 minutes, or until the tops are browned and firm.

Remove from oven, and cool completely before removing from pan. Slip a small knife in between each bagel and the edges of the pan to loosen each one before lifting out.

They're obviously not as robust as conventional wheat-based bagels, so handle with care. Slice them in half and fill with smoked salmon and cream cheese, fresh rocket or baby spinach or some crispy bacon and fried egg or whatever else lights you up. If you want to toast them, then pop them under the grill rather than in the toaster as they're a little too delicate for that!

BUTTERMILK BREAD

Makes 1 loaf

Ingredients

80 g almond meal
225 g coconut flour
70 g flax meal
10 g psyllium husk
25 g chia meal
1½ tablespoons sunflower seeds
1 tablespoon flax seed
1 teaspoon salt
1 teaspoon baking soda
½ teaspoon baking powder
500 ml buttermilk
3 free-range or pastured eggs
100 g unsalted butter, melted
100 ml filtered water

Instructions

Preheat oven to 350°F/180°C. Grease a large loaf tin well, especially in the corners (dust after greasing with a little extra coconut flour).

Add the dry ingredients to a mixing bowl and mix through so the psyllium and raising agents are mixed into the flours.

Beat the buttermilk, eggs and butter together.

Mix the wet into the dry ingredients and pour into the loaf tin. Top with some extra seeds.

Bake for 40–50 minutes until your bread is browned, firm and pulls away slightly from the edges.

Allow to cool. Serve.

You can slice the loaf and pack 2–3 slices as portions in the fridge for a few days or freeze them for later use. It is a super dense, nutrient-rich bread, so a little goes a long, long way!

NUT AND SEED BREAD

Makes 1 loaf

Ingredients

150 g almonds
100 g pecans
100 g macadamias
30 g hazelnuts
20 g pistachios (green)
50 g sunflower seeds
50 g flax seeds
50 g pumpkin seeds
50 g sesame seeds
3 whole free-range or pastured
    eggs
4 free-range or pastured egg whites
⅓ cup coconut oil (olive oil is a nice
    alternative)
A pinch of salt
1 tablespoon xylitol syrup (optional)

Instructions

Preheat oven to 325°F/160°C. Grease a loaf tin.

In a coffee grinder or food processor, grind seeds and half of the nuts to a coarse meal. Chop the other half of the nuts roughly so these give chunkier bits to the bread.

In a bowl combine all of the ingredients and stir well together. Spoon mixture into a loaf tin.

Bake for 50 minutes–1 hour. Allow to cool before removing from the pan.

The bread keeps moist and delicious up to a week in the fridge. You can also freeze it as well.

CHEESE BREAD

Makes 1 loaf

Ingredients

5 free-range or pastured egg whites

240 g almond meal

140 g coconut flour

20 g flax meal

1 teaspoon xanthan gum

4 teaspoons baking powder

¼ teaspoon salt

1½ cups grated mozzarella (or cheddar or pecorino)

¼ cup olive oil

1 sachet instant yeast (2 teaspoons of granules), dissolved in ¼ cup warm water

Instructions

Preheat oven to 350°F/180°C. Grease a large loaf tin.

Separate the eggs and beat the whites until frothy.

Mix the dry ingredients well together and then add the cheese. Add the olive oil to the yeast mixture and then add this wet mixture to the dry mix. Combine thoroughly. Fold in the egg whites gently so they don't lose their volume.

Place mixture in the tin and bake for 50 minutes or so until top is golden. Allow to cool in tin before turning out.

This is delicious with heaps of butter or topped with fresh avo mash seasoned with lemon juice, salt and pepper and a drizzle of peri peri or chilli-infused olive oil.

ZUCCHINI AND HAZELNUT BREAD

Makes 1 loaf

Ingredients

½ cup sesame seeds

½ cup sunflower seeds

½ cup pumpkin seeds

3 tablespoons psyllium husk
powder

1 teaspoon salt

½ teaspoon smoked paprika (or
straight up paprika if needs be)

2 large zucchini (baby marrows),
grated

⅓ cup hazelnuts, chopped

5 free-range or pastured eggs

3 tablespoons olive oil

½ cup cream

1 teaspoon baking powder

Instructions

Preheat oven to 350°F/180°C. Grease a loaf tin.

Mix all dry ingredients (other than baking powder) together well and then add the zucchini and hazelnuts.

Beat eggs, olive oil and cream well and then add this wet mixture to the dry ingredients. Add baking powder and stir through really well.

Spoon mixture into the tin and bake for 45–55 minutes until top is golden and the bread is pulling away from the sides.

Play around with different nuts – pecans are also great, and try adding a small bit of finely grated red onion for a slightly more punchy flavour.

'INCREDIBLE HULK' GREEN BREAD

Makes 1 loaf

Ingredients

1 cup sunflower seed butter

5 tablespoons coconut milk (you can substitute with full-cream cow's milk if you prefer)

1 tablespoon apple cider vinegar

1 tablespoon xylitol syrup

4 free-range or pastured eggs

3 tablespoons coconut flour

½ teaspoon salt

1 teaspoon baking soda

Instructions

Preheat oven to 320°F/160°C. Grease a loaf tin with coconut oil and line with baking paper (optional).

In a bowl combine the sunflower butter, milk, vinegar, xylitol and 1 egg and mix together well.

Crack the 3 remaining eggs into a separate bowl, and beat with an electric beater until thick and fluffy. Pour this over the sunflower butter mixture along with sifted coconut flour, salt and baking soda. Fold gently until it is well mixed (don't over-mix so you don't lose the aerated volume).

Pour into the loaf tin and bake for 45 minutes – until the crust is a deep brown and feels springy when lightly pressed.

Remove from the oven, allow to cool in the tin, then turn out onto a wire rack.

The green colour of the inside will deepen the more the bread cools. This is a fun bread for kids' sandwiches, and while it looks a little odd, it tastes fabulous.

AROUND-THE-WORLD FLATBREAD

Makes 2 small flatbreads

Ingredients

2 tablespoons coconut flour
2 tablespoons finely grated
   Parmesan
¼ teaspoon baking soda
¼ teaspoon baking powder
1 pinch of salt
Grinding of black pepper
1 pinch of any herbs on hand
   (optional)
2 large free-range or pastured eggs
4 tablespoons any kind of cream
   (diary or coconut)
1–2 tablespoons butter, for pan-
   frying

Instructions

Mix dry ingredients together. Beat egg with cream and then add this liquid to the dry mixture. Stir until there are no lumps.

Let it sit for a minute (the batter will get a little fluffier).

Melt butter in the pan, and pour two small sandwich-sized 'pancakes' into your pan on medium heat. It will only spread a little bit. When the tops start to bubble just a little and the bottom is golden brown, flip them both over and cook until that side is also golden.

Remove from heat and eat immediately, with a nice selection of Mediterranean roasted veg, marinated feta, etc. Alternatively you can top them with some grated cheese and a little chopped fresh chilli and then pop them under the grill until the cheese melts.

These breads become more and more crispy the more butter you pan-fry them in, so play around with how you get to the flavour and consistency that appeals most!

PIZZA PERFECT

Makes 2 pizzas

Ingredients

Pizza base

1 cup almond meal
1 cup coconut flour
½ cup arrowroot powder
2 teaspoons baking powder
1 teaspoon salt
Grinding of black pepper
1 teaspoon fresh or dried oregano
1 teaspoon fresh or dried basil
1 teaspoon fresh or dried marjoram
1 teaspoon fresh garlic, finely chopped
¼ cup olive oil
2 free-range or pastured eggs

Toppings

Homemade tomato 'sugo'/chopped
    tinned tomato
Fresh herbs and leaves (fresh basil/
    fresh rosemary/rocket/baby
    spinach)
Pitted olives/artichokes/roasted
    peppers/caramelised onion/pan-
    fried mushrooms/grilled zucchini/
    roasted aubergine chunks
Crispy bacon/pancetta/chorizo/cubed
    roast chicken
Grated mozzarella/Parmesan/
    pecorino/chèvre/gorgonzola, etc
Seasonings (fresh or dried chilli/
    paprika/a dash of Tabasco/extra
    olive oil/roasted garlic cloves)

Instructions

Preheat oven to 350°F/180°C. If you have a pizza stone use this, otherwise a terracotta tile works well too. Alternatively grease two large baking trays.

In a large mixing bowl, combine all of the pizza base ingredients and mix thoroughly until a dough forms. Roll into two balls, then place each on a baking tray.

Flatten the dough to a consistent thickness of just over half a centimetre, forming it into a rectangle or circle, depending on your preference.

Bake the dough for 20 minutes until it becomes a firm crust.

While the crust is baking, prepare your toppings. Get the kids/your other half /your gang involved with making lots of options, so everyone can create their own personalised pizza.

Put a small portion of the chopped tomato or sugo on the pizza, spreading it across the entire surface. Experiment – less sauce will yield a crispier pizza, more sauce will yield a softer pizza. *À chacun son goût.*

Add the toppings on top of the sauce, sprinkling the cheese and then goodies like chopped chilli on last so the colour pops out on top of the cheese.

Turn up the oven by another 50°F/20°C and bake the pizza again for around 15 minutes or until the cheese has melted nicely. Toss on some fresh rocket or baby spinach, slice into wedges if you intend to share, and serve!

TACO SHELLS AND TORTILLAS

Makes 10–12 tortillas

Ingredients

¾ cup flax meal
¼ cup coconut flour
1 cup almond meal
2 tablespoons whole psyllium husks
2 tablespoons chia meal
1 teaspoon salt
1 cup water, lukewarm
2 tablespoons melted butter, ghee
   or coconut oil

Seasonings (optional)
Paprika/chilli powder/onion
   powder/garlic powder or finely
   minced garlic/dried or fresh
   herbs/sundried tomato/pesto

Instructions

Place the flax meal, coconut flour, almond meal and psyllium husks into a bowl. For best results make sure you use whole husks, making the tortillas more compact and flexible.

Add salt, any of your favourite seasonings and the chia meal.

Pour in the water and mix until well combined using your hands. If needed, add a few extra tablespoons of water. Go gently however, as if you use too much, the dough will get too sticky and difficult to roll. Let it rest in the fridge or on the kitchen counter for up to an hour.

Remove from fridge and cut into 6 equal pieces. You will use the cut-offs to make the remaining 4 tortillas. Place a piece of the dough between two pieces of baking paper and roll out until it's very thin. Alternatively, use a non-stick silicon-covered roller and a silicon mat.

Use a 15–18-cm lid or bowl to cut out the tortilla. Repeat with the remaining dough and the cut-offs.

To make taco shells, cut small pieces of baking paper and place the tortillas on top. Hang these over 2 rows of the grid in the oven (so they will be wide enough to fit the filling inside) and turn the oven on. Cook until it reaches 200°C/400°F and then cook for further 5–8 minutes or until crispy.

To make tortillas, preheat a heavy-bottom pan greased with a bit of ghee or coconut oil. Place the tortilla into the hot pan and cook over a medium heat on each side for about 2 minutes until lightly browned. Don't overcook or they will be too crispy and will lose their flexibility. Grease more when needed and repeat for the rest of the tortillas. When done, leave them to cool.

To prevent them from getting too dry and hard, place in an airtight container and store for up to a week.

Tortilla bowls are a fun way to house a salad. To make these, preheat the oven to 200°C/400°F. Place the raw tortilla over a small heat-resistant bowl lined with baking paper and fold the edges round it to create a bowl shape. Lining the bowl is very important to prevent the dough from sticking. Place in the oven and bake for about 10 minutes until the top is lightly browned.

COCONUT AND CRANBERRY BREAD

Makes 1 loaf

Ingredients

160 g almond meal

30 g desiccated coconut

95 g coconut flour

¼ cup ground flax meal

¼ teaspoon salt

1 teaspoon ground cinnamon

1 teaspoon baking soda

½ teaspoon baking powder

6 free-range or pastured eggs

¼ cup oil (coconut or MCT)

1 tablespoon erythritol/xylitol
    granules

1 tablespoon apple cider vinegar

1 apple, grated

50 g dried or frozen cranberries

Additional flaked coconut for
    topping

Instructions

Preheat oven to 350°F/180°C. Grease a loaf tin well.

Place the almond meal, desiccated coconut, coconut flour, ground flax, salt, cinnamon, baking soda and baking powder in the bowl of a food processor and blitz to combine. Alternatively use a hand whisk.

Add the eggs, oil, sweetener and vinegar and pulse until a batter is formed. Add in the apple and cranberries.

Pour the batter into a prepared loaf tin and top with a little extra flaked coconut and a little extra sprinkle of cinnamon if desired.

Bake in the oven for 50 minutes until the loaf is cooked through. If you're unsure, insert a wooden skewer or toothpick in, and if it comes out clean, you know that the loaf is ready.

This is a great bread for a weekend treat. Play around with what you add in – pecans make a great combo with apple and cranberry.

FRESH GINGER LOAF

Makes 1 loaf

Ingredients

120 g fresh ginger, peeled and
    grated or minced
¾ cup xylitol syrup
3 large free-range or pastured eggs
½ cup macadamia oil
Zest of one orange
2 teaspoons pure vanilla extract
1½ cups almond meal
½ cup coconut flour
½ cup flax meal
½ teaspoon salt
1 teaspoon baking soda
1 teaspoon ground cinnamon
½ teaspoon ground cloves
½ teaspoon freshly grated nutmeg
Grinding of black pepper

Instructions

Preheat oven to 350°F/180°C. Grease a 22x12-cm loaf tin with melted butter or a little coconut oil.

Combine the ginger, xylitol syrup, eggs, oil, zest and vanilla in a food processor or mixing bowl and whisk.

Place the flours in a bowl and add the salt, baking soda, cinnamon, cloves, nutmeg and pepper, combining all well. Add the wet ingredients to the almond meal mixture and mix until really smooth.

If you don't have a processor, just whisk the dry ingredients together in a mixing bowl. Then whisk the wet ingredients into the dry ingredients but the bread is a little lighter and tenderer if made in a blender.

Pour into the prepared tin and bake for 1 hour. After 35–40 minutes, lightly place a piece of foil over the bread to keep it from getting too brown on top. Let it cool in the pan for 45–60 minutes. Cut into thick slices with a serrated knife. Good on its own, but even better with lashings of butter!

COOKIES AND TREATS

COCONUT MACAROONS

Makes 16 macaroons

Ingredients

2 large free-range or pastured egg
    whites
¼ cup xylitol syrup
¼ teaspoon salt
2½ cups coconut flakes

Instructions

Preheat oven to 350°F/180°C. Grease a baking tray well.

In a medium-sized bowl, whisk together egg whites and xylitol syrup with a fork. Add in the salt, then stir in the coconut flakes.

Place the bowl in the fridge to chill for ½ hour.

Using a tablespoon-sized measuring spoon, scoop up some mixture so that the spoon is heaped full. Then, using your hand, firmly pack the mixture into the scoop so it is level.

Invert the spoon and tap to release the scoop onto the baking tray. Do the same with the rest of the mixture, locating the macaroons a few centimetres apart from one another.

Bake for 10–12 minutes, until macaroons are golden brown.

Allow to cool completely before serving so that they are crisp. Store in an airtight container.

CHOCOLATE GANACHE THUMBPRINT COOKIES

Makes approximately 16 cookies

Ingredients

Cookies

1 cup roasted macadamia nuts

1 cup unsweetened shredded
  coconut

¼ cup coconut flour

1 teaspoon vanilla extract

¼ cup coconut oil melted

1 tablespoon xylitol syrup

2 free-range or pastured eggs

½ teaspoon orange zest

Chocolate ganache

3 tablespoons coconut oil melted

2 tablespoons xylitol syrup

1 tablespoon unsweetened cocoa
  powder

2 teaspoons arrowroot powder

Instructions

Preheat oven to 350°F/180°C. Grease a baking tray
with butter.

Place the macadamia nuts in a food processor and
pulse into a coarse meal (but not so much to make
butter).

Add the coconut, coconut flour, vanilla, coconut oil,
xylitol syrup, eggs and orange zest and pulse until well
combined, about 30 seconds.

Scoop up tablespoons of dough and roll into ball
shapes, placing these onto the baking tray. Press your
thumb into each ball to create a well (if the dough is
too soft, put in the fridge for 15 minutes or until the
cookies firm up).

Bake for 20 minutes. Set aside to cool.

Mix ganache ingredients together so mixture is totally
smooth. Spoon a little into the centre well of each
cookie.

Garnish with extra orange zest.

CHOCCA MOCHA COOKIES

Makes 16 cookies

Ingredients

¼ cup melted butter or coconut oil

⅓ cup cocoa powder

3 large free-range or pastured eggs

⅓ cup erythritol/xylitol granules

¼ teaspoon salt

¼ teaspoon vanilla extract

¼ cup sifted coconut flour

¾ teaspoon finely ground espresso beans

Raw cacao nibs or chopped pecans (optional)

Instructions

Preheat oven to 350°F/180°C. Grease a baking tray well with butter or coconut oil.

In a saucepan at low heat, melt butter and stir in cocoa powder. Whisk well so that there are no lumps, then remove from heat and let cool.

In a bowl, combine eggs, sweetener, salt and vanilla, mixing well to combine thoroughly.

Stir in cocoa mixture.

Whisk coconut flour and espresso beans into batter until there are no lumps.

Let batter rest for 4–5 minutes to allow it to thicken slightly.

Drop batter by the spoonful onto the greased baking tray. Sprinkle each cookie with a few cacao nibs or chopped pecans if using.

Bake for 14 minutes until golden. Allow to cool completely. Store in an airtight container. Dust with extra cocoa before serving.

ORANGE AND POPPY SEED SHORTBREAD

Makes 20–24 shortbread cookies

Ingredients

170 g almond meal

110 g coconut flour

10 g chia meal

40 g poppy seeds

½ teaspoon salt

¼ cup xylitol syrup

½ cup butter (cold, cut into small pieces)

1 tablespoon orange zest

1 teaspoon vanilla extract

Instructions

Preheat oven to 350°F/180°C.

In a large bowl, whisk together the almond meal, coconut flour, chia meal, poppy seeds and salt.

Add xylitol syrup and mix through well.

Add butter pieces, orange zest and vanilla.

With a pastry blade in your food processor, or with your hands, combine ingredients until they form small crumbs. The dough should stick together if you pinch it between two fingers.

Lay out a long piece of parchment and dump the crumbly dough into the centre. Cover with another piece of parchment paper and then roll out until about 4 mm thick.

Cut out squares, rounds or stars with a cookie cutter. Using a metal lifter, transfer the shortbread cookies to a well-greased baking tray. The thinner they are, the crispier they'll get, but a deep piece of shortbread is also delicious, so play around with the depth of the dough and bake off a few alternatives before baking the whole mixture.

Bake for 12 minutes, or until the edges are lightly browned. Remove from the oven and allow to cool. Store in an airtight container.

COCONUT TRAIL-MIX COOKIES

Makes 20–24 cookies

Ingredients

40 g sunflower seeds

40 g green pumpkin seeds

40 g chopped almonds

40 g chopped macadamias

½ cup coconut flour, sifted

1½ cups unsweetened desiccated
    coconut

½ cup of oil (coconut or MCT)

½ cup of xylitol syrup

¼ teaspoon salt

4 free-range or pastured eggs

¾ teaspoon almond extract

Instructions

Preheat oven to 350°F/180°C. Grease a baking tray well.

Mix seeds and nuts together and set aside.

In a large bowl blend coconut flour and desiccated coconut completely. Mix in your trail mix, using a fork to keep it fluffy.

In a separate bowl, combine coconut oil, xylitol syrup, salt, eggs and almond extract, and blend until consistency is smooth.

Combine the wet ingredients with the dry ingredients. Mix well, folding the flour mixture into the batter over and over. Keep at it to ensure all the ingredients are well integrated. Allow to rest for 5 minutes in the fridge.

Using 2 teaspoons, scrape up the dough into balls and place on the baking tray. They won't spread much, but you'll need about 4 cm between them. Using a fork gently press the cookies down. Lie the fork into the dough in one direction, and then the other, if you like, so you have a little chequered pattern.

Pop the baking tray into the oven and bake for 10–12 minutes. Check them occasionally and take them out when they just start to brown on the tips. Store in an airtight container.

TAHINI SESAME COOKIES

Makes approximately 30 cookies

Ingredients

1 cup tahini, stirred well
1 cup erythritol/xylitol granules
1 large free-range or pastured egg
1 teaspoon baking soda
¼ teaspoon salt
¼ cup sesame seeds

Instructions

Preheat oven to 350°F/180°C.

Beat tahini, sweetener, egg, baking soda and salt together to combine well.

Roll tablespoons of dough into balls, dampening your hands with water to prevent sticking.

Place balls about 5 cm apart on ungreased baking trays. Flatten slightly by making cross-hatches on top with the tines of a fork. Sprinkle tops with sesame seeds.

Bake cookies for about 12 minutes, until golden on the bottom but still soft in the centre. Cool on the baking trays for 5 minutes. Transfer to wire racks to cool completely.

These totally flourless cookies have an amazing nutty taste, kind of like a cross between halva and peanut butter cookies.

GINGER 'TREACLE' COOKIES

Makes approximately 12 cookies

Ingredients

3 tablespoons flax meal, soaked in
   3 tablespoons warm water
½ cup almond meal
⅓ cup coconut flour
2 tablespoons chia meal
¼ teaspoon salt
½ teaspoon baking soda
1 teaspoon ground cinnamon
2 teaspoons ground ginger
½ teaspoon ground cloves
⅓ cup erythritol/xylitol granules
¼ cup coconut oil
1 tablespoon xylitol syrup

Instructions

Preheat oven to 350°F/180°C. Grease a baking tray with coconut oil or butter.

In a small separate bowl, mix together the flax meal and warm water and let it sit until it thickens and gels.

In a large mixing bowl or food processor mix together all the dry ingredients.

Melt the coconut oil, then place it along with the flax mixture and the xylitol syrup into the bowl or food processor and mix well. Adding some very finely chopped fresh ginger adds a wonderful zing.

Place the dough on a silicon mat or between two pieces of greaseproof paper and roll out. Cut out shapes with a cookie cutter. Alternatively, take a little bit of the dough and roll it into a ball, then press down onto the baking tray, flattening it with a fork if you like to add some surface detail.

Repeat with the balance of dough and then bake for about 10–15 minutes. Let cool before serving.

CHOCOLATE GINGERBREAD MEN

Makes a village of gingerbread men

Ingredients

⅔ cup almond meal
⅓ cup coconut flour, sifted
¼ cup cocoa powder, sifted
⅔ cup erythritol/xylitol granules
1 teaspoon baking soda
1½ teaspoon ground ginger
1 teaspoon cinnamon
¼ teaspoon nutmeg
⅛ teaspoon salt
2 free-range or pastured eggs,
    beaten
⅓ cup melted butter or coconut oil
2 tablespoons xylitol syrup
1 teaspoon vanilla extract

Instructions

Preheat oven to 350°F/180°C. Line baking trays with parchment paper.

In a large mixing bowl combine almond meal, coconut flour, cocoa powder, sweetener, baking soda, ground ginger, cinnamon, nutmeg and salt. Mix together thoroughly.

In a medium-sized mixing bowl combine eggs, melted butter or coconut oil, xylitol syrup and vanilla extract. Mix together well. Add egg mixture to flour mixture and combine thoroughly.

Once dough is thoroughly mixed, place bowl of dough in freezer for 8 minutes. Remove from freezer and place between two sheets of parchment paper. Roll dough into a flat rectangle that will fit on your baking tray.

Peel away top parchment paper slowly and press out gingerbread men with your cookie cutter, gently lifting the men onto a well-greased baking tray. Use up remaining pastry by balling together, rolling the dough out again and cutting as many more men as your size cutter delivers. Your yield will depend on the size of your cutter.

Bake for 10–15 minutes, checking at 10 minutes, or until browned. Remove baking tray from oven and let cool completely before moving as they're not as robust as the little men containing gluten!

COCONUT AND MACADAMIA COOKIES

Makes 20 cookies

Ingredients

½ cup coconut oil (melted butter or
    MCT oil may be substituted)
½ cup erythritol/xylitol granules
2 free-range or pastured eggs
½ teaspoon vanilla extract
⅛ teaspoon salt
1 cup coconut flour
½ cup unsweetened desiccated
    coconut
½ cup macadamia nuts, coarsely
    chopped
½ cup raw cacao nibs

Instructions

Preheat oven to 350°F/180°C. Grease a baking tray.

Mix the coconut oil, sweetener, eggs and vanilla with a hand mixer, stick blender or in a food processor.

Add coconut flour and mix well, then add coconut, macadamia nuts and cacao nibs. Stir gently to combine.

Scoop cookies onto the baking tray. They won't spread or rise very much, so you can place them fairly close together.

Bake for about 15 minutes, until nicely golden brown. Allow to cool and enjoy!

You could substitute the cacao nibs for dried cranberries or use pecans instead of macs.

SQUARES AND BARS

BROWNIES WITH GOJI BERRIES

Makes 8 brownies

Ingredients

160 g of butter

½ cup of cocoa powder

3 free-range or pastured eggs,
    beaten

4 tablespoons cream

¼ cup almond meal

¼ cup coconut flour

2 tablespoons flax meal

½ teaspoon xanthan gum

½ teaspoon baking powder

½ cup erythritol/xylitol granules

50 g gojis (or cranberries, pecans or
    hazels – they're all good)

Instructions

Preheat oven to 350°F/180°C. Grease a square or rectangular baking pan or ceramic dish. Keep the pan size smaller rather than larger as these brownies are much nicer when they are deeper, rather than bigger and thinner, so to speak.

Melt the butter and then sift the cocoa over it, mixing until both are thoroughly combined and the mixture has no lumps.

Beat the eggs then add the cream and mix thoroughly.

In a separate bowl, mix all the dry ingredients together and then add the wet to the dry, mixing thoroughly. Stir through the goji berries, distributing evenly.

Spoon mixture into the baking dish and bake for 30 minutes. Cool for 10 minutes before slicing. Store in the fridge but allow to come to room temperature before serving so the fats soften, releasing the full flavour of the brownie.

CHEESECAKE SWIRL BROWNIES

Makes 16 brownies

Ingredients

Brownie batter

1½ cups almond meal

½ cup coconut flour

½ cup plus 1 tablespoon unsweetened cocoa powder (or raw cacao powder)

2 teaspoons baking powder

1 teaspoon baking soda

4 tablespoons erythritol/xylitol granules

5 large free-range or pastured eggs

2 teaspoons vanilla extract

3 tablespoons heavy cream

2 tablespoons strong brewed coffee, at room temperature (or extra coconut milk or cream)

½ cup unsalted butter, melted

Cheesecake batter

250 g cream cheese at room temperature

4 tablespoons butter at room temperature

1 teaspoon vanilla extract

½ cup erythritol/xylitol granules

2 large free-range or pastured eggs

Instructions

Preheat oven to 350°F/180°C. Grease a 20x20-cm pan with butter or coconut oil.

For the brownie batter, place dry ingredients in a medium bowl and blend well with a whisk.

Add the remaining ingredients and mix with a wooden spoon so that the mixture is smooth.

For cheesecake batter, beat the cream cheese and butter together until smooth.

Add vanilla and sweetener and beat well. Add the two eggs and beat until well combined.

Spread half the brownie batter into the bottom of the prepared pan. Next, carefully pour on the cream cheese mixture and spread to cover the chocolate. Then drop heaped tablespoons of the reserved brownie batter over the top of cream cheese. Use a knife to cut through the chocolate just into the cream cheese layer to swirl and 'marbleise' the batter.

Bake for 30-odd minutes, depending on how moist you like your brownies. Do not overbake or you'll dry them out!

Allow to cool in the pan, then slice into squares. Store in the fridge.

BLUEBERRY COCONUT SQUARES

Makes approximately 12 squares

Ingredients

¼ cup unsweetened apple sauce
⅓ cup coconut oil, melted
4 free-range or pastured eggs
3–4 tablespoons xylitol syrup
1 tablespoon vanilla extract
½ cup coconut flour
1 tablespoon cinnamon
¼ teaspoon baking soda
⅔ cup blueberries

Instructions

Preheat oven to 325°F/160°C. Grease a 33x22-cm or 20x20-cm baking dish or pan that is at least 4 cm in height up the sides.

Mix apple sauce, coconut oil, eggs, xylitol syrup and vanilla extract in a small bowl.

Stir in coconut flour, cinnamon and baking soda.

Fold in the blueberries.

Distribute the batter evenly in the pan. Sprinkle a little more cinnamon and 2 teaspoons of raw coconut sugar on top of the batter before baking for a lovely crunchy 'crust' if you like.

Bake for 35–40 minutes. Allow to cool in the pan before cutting into squares and removing. Store in the fridge, but allow to come to room temperature before serving as this 'releases' the fats and opens up the flavour.

SHORTBREAD SQUARES WITH SALTED CARAMEL GLAZE

Makes approximately 16 squares

Ingredients

Shortbread

1¾ cups almond meal

¼ cup coconut flour

½ teaspoon salt

¼ cup xylitol syrup

½ cup butter, cold and cut into
   small pieces

1 teaspoon vanilla extract

Salted caramel

1 cup heavy cream

½ teaspoon salt

¾ cup xylitol syrup

Maldon or any other kind of
   flaked salt for topping

Instructions

Preheat oven to 350°F/180°C.

Whisk together the almond meal, coconut flour and salt in a large bowl.

Pour xylitol syrup over the dry mixture and stir through. Add butter pieces and vanilla. With a pastry blade in your food processor, or with your hands, combine ingredients until they form small crumbs. The dough should stick together if you pinch some in-between two fingers.

Lay out a long piece of parchment paper and turn out the dough into the centre. Cover with another piece of parchment paper, and roll the dough out into a long rectangle. Using the pizza cutter or a knife, cut the rectangle lengthwise in half, then cut across both ways into squares. Using the small spatula, transfer the squares to a parchment-lined baking tray, or press the dough directly into a well-greased baking tray and score with a knife.

Bake for 12 minutes, or until the edges are lightly browned. Remove from oven and immediately slide parchment to a wire rack. Let cool completely before dipping into caramel.

Prepare a shallow pie plate or round ceramic container by filling it halfway with cold water. Set aside.

To prepare the caramel, heat the cream and salt over a medium heat in a small saucepan until bubbles start to form along the edges of the pan. Add the xylitol syrup and stir until completely heated through.

Turn the heat up and bring the mixture to a boil. Attach a candy thermometer to the side of the pan (if you have one), taking care that it does not touch the bottom of the pan. Lower the heat to medium to keep the mixture at a slow simmer. Stirring constantly with a wooden spoon, cook the mixture for 15–20 minutes or until it reaches 255°F/120°C. Turn off the heat.

Carefully lower the saucepan into the container filled halfway with cold water. Mix with a wooden spoon as the caramel cools and thickens. Tilt the saucepan to the side so that the caramel pools on one side. Dip the cooled shortbread bars halfway into the caramel and then place on a parchment-lined baking tin and sprinkle with salt flakes immediately. Transfer the baking tin to the fridge to harden completely. Store in an airtight container.

CRANBERRY ENERGY BARS

Makes 8 bars

Ingredients

¼ cup almonds

¼ cup Brazil nuts

¼ cup green pumpkin seeds

¼ cup sunflower seeds

¼ cup unsweetened desiccated
coconut

¼ cup oil (coconut or MCT)

¼ cup crunchy almond butter
(you could use any nut or seed
butter)

1 teaspoon raw honey (optional but
it helps hold them together)

1½ teaspoons vanilla extract

½ teaspoon salt

¼ cup flax meal

½ cup pure whey isolate protein
powder

1 large free-range or pastured egg

⅓ cup dried cranberries

¼ cup unsweetened flaked coconut
to sprinkle on top

Instructions

Preheat oven to 350°F/180°C. Grease a small square pan or a regular loaf tin.

On a baking tray, toast nuts, seeds, and desiccated coconut until golden, raking the tray halfway through for even toasting. Allow to cool.

Pour mixture into a food processor and pulse until nuts are chopped and the mixture becomes coarsely ground (keeping some larger chunks for texture).

In a small pot, melt the oil, almond butter and honey over a low heat, stirring well to combine. Remove from heat and add vanilla extract and salt.

Pour wet ingredients into nut mixture, and then add the flax meal and protein powder, mixing thoroughly until combined.

Beat the egg in the bowl you used for your wet ingredients, then add that to the mixture and combine thoroughly.

Fold in the berries until well incorporated.

Press mixture into the pan and top with the coconut flakes.

Bake for 12 minutes. Remove from the oven. Let cool for 15 minutes, then cut into 8 portions using a sharp knife. Store in an airtight container. These make great 'emergency rations' to keep in the car or your desk!

APPLE AND NUT SQUARES

Makes 12 squares

Ingredients

Crust
3 free-range or pastured egg yolks
2 tablespoons xylitol syrup
3 tablespoons ghee, butter or
    coconut oil
¼ teaspoon baking soda
½ cup coconut flour
¼ cup water

Apple layer
3 apples, cut into small dice
1 tablespoon erythritol/xylitol
    granules
50 ml water
⅛ teaspoon pectin

Nut/seed topping
1½ cups nuts (preferably soaked
    and dehydrated) – mix ½ cup
    pecans, ½ cup almonds and
    ½ cup pumpkin seeds
3 free-range or pastured egg whites
½ cup erythritol/xylitol granules

Instructions

Preheat oven to 350°F/180°C. Grease and flour a 20×20-cm pan.

For the crust, beat the egg yolks until frothy, then add xylitol and ghee (or other fat).

Stir the baking soda into the coconut flour, then stir dry mixture into wet mixture.

Add water and mix until combined.

Scatter the crust mixture throughout the pan by dolloping the mixture with a spoon, then use your hands to spread and press down the dough evenly.

For the apple mixture, place the chopped apple in a small pot with the water and sweetener and cook until the apple softens. Add the pectin and cook until all the water is absorbed. Allow to cool.

Spread the apple mixture across the dough.

Grind nuts and seeds in a coffee-bean grinder or processor into a coarse meal.

Whip egg whites until stiff. Add sweetener and whip further, then add the nut and seed meal.

Spread egg white mixture over the apple mixture and then bake for 20 minutes or until the meringue top is golden. Cool before cutting.

BANTING 'TOP DECK' BARS

Makes 12 bars

Ingredients

Base

½ cup almonds
½ cup macadamias
½ cup sunflower seeds
½ cup pumpkin seeds
½ cup flax meal
½ cup desiccated coconut
½ cup almond butter
¼ teaspoon salt
½ cup coconut oil, melted (feel free
    to use cocoa butter or butter for
    a warmer weather-stable bar)
2 tablespoons xylitol syrup
1 tablespoon pure whey isolate
    protein powder
2 teaspoons vanilla extract

Topping

½ teaspoon ground cinnamon
4 tablespoons coconut oil, melted
    (or MCT oil)
1 teaspoon vanilla extract
1 tablespoon xylitol syrup
4 tablespoons cocoa powder or
    raw cacao

Instructions

Grease a 20x20-cm square pan.

Place nuts and seeds, flax meal, coconut, almond butter and salt in the bowl of a food processor and blend until the nuts and seeds are ground into a coarse meal.

Melt the coconut oil over a low heat if solid and then add sweetener, whey and vanilla to bowl and process until well combined to form a thick, yet crunchy paste.

Press the mixture into the pan – a larger pan will produce thinner bars, while a smaller pan will yield deeper ones, so use what you have and play around to find the depth you like most. Place in the fridge to chill.

While bars are chilling, prepare the chocolate 'deck' topping by warming the cinnamon in a pot with the coconut oil. Add the vanilla, xylitol syrup and sifted cocoa/cacao and stir through well to remove any lumps that may form. Allow to simmer very gently for a few minutes to thicken slightly, then remove from heat and allow to cool down completely.

Top the bars with the sauce and return to the fridge to set. Cut into squares and serve. The chocolate topping does soften at room temperature so store these in the fridge and remove just before serving.

Note: These are obviously not 'baked' as such, but they had to be included in this collection of recipes. You can trade out some of the flax meal for extra whey isolate powder to up the protein levels. Play around with different nut-and-seed combinations to see how the flavour changes and which combination really lights you up!

CAKES AND CUPCAKES

PUMPKIN CHEESECAKE CUPS

Makes 12 cups

Ingredients

Crust

½ cup pecans

½ cup almonds

3 tablespoons coconut oil (or butter or ghee), melted

1 tablespoon xylitol syrup

1 teaspoon pure vanilla extract

½ teaspoon cinnamon

¼ teaspoon baking soda

¼ teaspoon salt

Pumpkin pie layer

1 cup roasted pumpkin purée (see page 34)

1 free-range or pastured egg

1½ teaspoons pumpkin pie spice

1 tablespoon erythritol/xylitol granules

Whipped cheesecake topping

240 g cream cheese

120 g butter

1 tablespoon pure vanilla extract

½ teaspoon pumpkin pie spice or cinnamon

Extra pecans and almonds, chopped

Instructions

Preheat oven to 350°F/180°C. Line a cupcake pan with 12 cupcake liners.

Grind the pecans and almonds to somewhere just south of a fine flour so some coarser chunks remain.

Make your crust by combining all the ingredients until well mixed. Press about a teaspoon of the nut mixture into the bottom of each cupcake liner. Bake for 8–10 minutes. Allow to cool.

Mix your pumpkin pie layer by combining all the ingredients. Put about 1 tablespoon of the pumpkin pie mixture on top of the nut base. Bake for 45 minutes or until set. Allow to cool.

For the topping, mix all ingredients for a few minutes until smooth and creamy. Add your cheesecake topping on top of the pumpkin pie layer by filling the cups until the cheesecake mixture reaches the top. Add some extra chopped nuts on top of the cheesecake layer.

For a more 'adult' version, skip the cupcake liners and press the nut crust into a well-greased rectangular baking dish and then proceed with the layers. Cut into squares for a tea-time treat or as a dessert!

STRAWBERRY CUPCAKES

Makes 6 cupcakes

Ingredients

Cupcakes

3 tablespoons butter, melted

3 free-range of pastured eggs

3 tablespoons erythritol/xylitol granules

¼ teaspoon salt

¼ teaspoon vanilla

¼ cup sifted coconut flour

¼ teaspoon baking powder

Strawberry purée

200 g fresh strawberries

3 tablespoons water

5 ml lemon juice

1 tablespoon erythritol/xylitol granules

Instructions

Preheat oven to 350°F/180°C. Grease your muffin tin or muffin liners well.

Blend together the butter, eggs, sweetener, salt and vanilla.

Combine coconut flour with baking powder and whisk into a batter until there are no lumps. Pour batter into the greased muffin cups. It's even more delicious if you add some chopped fresh strawberries into the batter, by the way!

Bake for 15 minutes. Allow to cool.

For the strawberry purée, cut the strawberries into chunks and then simmer gently in the water to which you've added the lemon juice and sweetener. Cook down until the water has absorbed and the berries are soft. Allow to cool, then purée in a blender until smooth.

Serve the cupcakes topped with fresh strawberries and whipped cream or with mascarpone drizzled with strawberry purée.

BAKED BERRY CHEESECAKE

Makes 1 cheesecake

Ingredients

Crust

2 large free-range or pastured
    eggs, beaten till frothy
1 cup almond meal
⅓ cup erythritol/xylitol granules
1 teaspoon baking powder

Filling

500 g thick cream cheese
80 ml erythritol/xylitol granules
10 ml fine orange zest
80 ml orange juice
3 free-range or pastured eggs
5 ml vanilla extract
250 ml cream, whipped
150 g blueberries, frozen
Additional fresh blueberries or
    fresh strawberries to decorate

Instructions

Preheat oven to 350°F/180°C. Grease a 20-cm
spring-form pan with butter.

For the crust, combine all the ingredients and mix well.
Pour into the greased dish, spread evenly across the
bottom and bake in the oven for 15 minutes or until
lightly browned. Allow to cool for 5 minutes.

For the filling, beat the cream cheese and sweetener
until smooth and creamy.

Gradually beat in the orange zest and juice. Add the
eggs and vanilla and beat until combined.

Fold in the whipped cream. Add in the blueberries and
mix again. Pour the mixture onto the cooled base.

Wrap the tin in foil and then place it into a roasting
pan and pour in water to come halfway up the sides of
the tin.

Bake for 30–40 minutes or until the filling is set but still
has a slight wobble in the middle.

Switch off the oven and open the door slightly. Allow
to cool in the oven for an hour. Remove and refrigerate
until well chilled.

Top with additional berries or serve with a berry
compote.

CHOCOLATE PUMPKIN SEED FLOUR CAKE

Makes 1 cake

Ingredients

2 cups pumpkin seed flour
¾ cup cocoa powder
¼ cup arrowroot powder
1¼ teaspoons baking soda
¼ teaspoon salt
3 large free-range or pastured eggs
⅔ cup xylitol syrup
⅓ cup fruity olive or coconut oil
1¼ cups coconut milk
2 teaspoons vanilla

Instructions

Preheat oven to 350°F/180°C. Grease a 20-cm round springform cake pan.

In a large mixing bowl whisk together the pumpkin seed flour, cocoa powder, arrowroot powder, baking soda and salt.

In a separate bowl, whisk together the eggs, xylitol syrup, oil, coconut milk and vanilla. Pour the wet ingredients into the dry and whisk together well.

Pour batter into prepared pan. Place the pan on the centre rack in the oven and bake for approximately 40 minutes. Test after about 35 minutes. If the top of the cake feels jiggly to the touch, it needs more time, if not, pull it out.

Cool for about 30 minutes in the pan, then run a knife around the edge of the pan and flip the cake onto a wire rack to cool. Best served slightly warm or at room temperature.

This rich, dark chocolate cake is high in protein and nutrients like zinc and essential fatty acids (linoleic and oleic fatty acids). Because of its richness, serve it with something slightly acidic such as fresh strawberries or homemade berry purée.

APPLE AND CRANBERRY UPSIDE-DOWN CAKE

Makes 1 cake

Ingredients

1½ cups coconut flour

1 cup almond meal

½ teaspoon salt

2 teaspoons ground cinnamon

2 cups full-fat coconut milk

1 cup xylitol syrup (divided)

12 free-range or pastured eggs, beaten

2 teaspoons vanilla extract

½ cup frozen cranberries

¼ cup coconut oil

50 ml lemon juice

5 apples, cored and cut into thin rounds

Instructions

Preheat oven to 350°F/180°C. Grease a 23-cm springform pan well.

Whisk coconut flour, almond meal, salt and cinnamon together.

Beat in coconut milk, ¾ of the xylitol syrup, eggs and vanilla and continue to beat them together until no clumps remain. Then add in half of the cranberries and mix through well.

Melt coconut oil in a 23-cm cast-iron skillet over a moderately high heat. Whisk in remaining xylitol syrup and lemon juice and simmer until these begin to foam and bubble. Pour the mixture into the bottom of the pan.

Arrange the apples in an overlapping fashion along the base of the pan. Sprinkle over the rest of the cranberries into the pan. Pour in the cake batter over the apple and cranberry. Bake for 45–60 minutes or until a toothpick inserted into the centre of the cake comes out clean.

Allow the cake to cool for about 5–10 minutes before inverting on a platter and serving. Decorate with extra cranberries and flaked coconut if you wish.

BAKED DESSERTS

CINNAMON APPLE TART WITH PECAN CRUST

Serves 8–10

Ingredients

Pecan tart crust
1½ cups pecans
1 free-range or pastured egg
1 tablespoon coconut flour
Pinch of salt

Filling
6–8 medium red apples, cored and
    sliced into 3 mm wafers
1 tablespoon fresh lemon juice
1 tablespoon arrowroot powder
2 tablespoon erythritol/xylitol
    granules
2 tablespoons coconut oil
1½ teaspoons ground ginger
Pinch of ground cloves
1 tablespoon ground cinnamon
    plus extra for sprinkling
1 free-range or pastured egg
60 ml cream

Instructions

Preheat the oven to 350°F/180°C. Grease a 20-cm loose-bottomed quiche/tart pan.

For the crust, place pecans in a food processor and pulse until quite fine. Then add in egg, coconut flour and salt, and pulse again until the mixture forms a ball.

Press crust onto bottom and up the sides of tart pan.

For the filling, toss apple slices, lemon juice, arrowroot, 1 tablespoon of the sweetener and spices in a large bowl.

Melt 2 tablespoons of the oil in a frying pan and then tip the apple mixture in, stirring well over a medium heat so the spices are well distributed and the apple slices soften, releasing some of their juices, and the sweetener granules melt.

Allow to cool and then fan the apple pieces on top of the uncooked crust, forming concentric circles, with 2–3 layers.

Beat the egg and then add the cream, mixing these well. Drizzle this over the fanned apple mixture. Sprinkle over a little extra cinnamon and the second tablespoon of sweetener.

Cover tart with foil, and bake for about 45–50 minutes, or until juices are bubbling. Then remove the foil and cook uncovered for 5–10 more minutes to crisp the top.

Serve with whipped cream, mascarpone or whipped coconut cream.

CHOCOLATE BROWNIE 'TRIFLE' WITH PUMPKIN CUSTARD

Serves 8

Ingredients

Brownies
150 g butter
½ cup cocoa powder
3 free-range or pastured eggs, beaten
3 tablespoons cream
½ cup almond meal
1 tablespoon flax meal
½ teaspoon baking powder
¼ teaspoon baking soda
½ cup erythritol/xylitol granules
60 g chopped pecans/walnuts

Custard
400 ml full-fat coconut milk
3 free-range or pastured egg yolks
⅓ cup xylitol syrup, melted
¼ cup pumpkin purée (see page 34)
1 teaspoon vanilla extract
½ teaspoon cinnamon
¼ teaspoon nutmeg
⅛ teaspoon ground cloves
⅛ teaspoon ginger
Pinch of salt

Instructions

For the brownies, preheat the oven to 350°F/180°C. Grease a baking dish.

Melt the butter and mix in the cocoa powder until it is completely smooth. Mix eggs and cream together well, then add the butter/cocoa mixture to the egg and cream mixture.

Mix all dry ingredients together, then add wet to dry and stir through well to combine evenly.

Spoon mixture into baking dish. Keep the dish deeper rather than wider so the brownies are thicker rather than thinner (batter should be about 4 cm deep).

Bake for 30 minutes. Cool for 10 minutes. Allow to cool, then cut into cubes.

For the custard, warm the coconut milk over a medium heat. Beat the egg yolks. Pour the warmed (but not boiling or you will curdle the egg) coconut milk into the egg yolks, whisking constantly. Then add the xylitol syrup (if you don't have this, use erythritol granules and melt this gently into the milk before adding the egg).

Add pumpkin purée, vanilla extract, spices and just a tiny pinch of salt and whisk thoroughly. Alternatively, put the mixture into the food processor (or use a stick blender) and blend until completely smooth and creamy.

Arrange some brownie cubes in a glass serving bowl or individually in some pretty glasses, then spoon over some custard, then add another layer of brownies, then more custard. Top with extra chopped pecans and strawberries or flaked coconut.

APPLE AND RASPBERRY CRUMBLE

Serves 6

Ingredients

Filling

5 red apples, chopped into bite-
size chunks
225 g fresh or frozen raspberries
(defrosted and drained)
1 teaspoon cinnamon
Juice of half a lemon
Knob of butter
30 ml filtered water

Topping

100 g almonds
100 g pecans
30 g desiccated coconut
30 g coconut flakes
½ cup erythritol/xylitol granules
1 teaspoon cinnamon
½ teaspoon ground ginger
75 ml coconut or MCT oil or butter
or ghee, melted

Instructions

Preheat oven to 350°F/180°C. Grease 6 individual small ramekins or an oven-proof casserole dish.

In a large bowl, toss the first four filling ingredients together.

Melt the knob of butter in a pot and then add the apple mixture, stirring through well to coat the mixture as evenly as possible. Allow the cinnamon to release its aroma and then add the water and cover the pot for a few minutes so that it steams and softens the apple chunks slightly. Allow to cool.

For the topping, pulse all the dry ingredients in a food processor until the nuts are chopped small, but not finely ground. Then add the oil and mix through thoroughly.

Divide the fruit mixture evenly across the ramekins or the base of the casserole dish so that they are about ¾ full (they will bake down quite a bit). Top the base mixture with the nut mixture and press down.

Bake for about 30 minutes, or until the top is golden and the fruit is soft.

Serve with whipped cream or coconut cream.

Whipped coconut cream is quite easy to make – place a can of coconut cream in the fridge overnight or into the freezer for about 2 hours. Chill a metal bowl in the freezer with the beaters for 30 minutes ahead of making. Beat the cream on high until peaks form, for about 2–3 minutes. Add a teaspoon of powdered erythritol or xylitol syrup at the end, keeping the beaters running. Serve immediately or store in the fridge and then beat again briefly before serving.

FRESH LIME CHEESECAKE TART

Serves 10–12

Ingredients

Crust

1 cup erythritol/xylitol granules
  (best ground into a finer form in
  the blender)
¾ cup almond meal
½ cup coconut flour
1½ teaspoons cinnamon
6 tablespoons butter, softened

Filling

250 g cream cheese, softened
1 teaspoon vanilla extract
½ cup fresh lime juice
3 free-range or pastured eggs
Lime zest

Instructions

Preheat oven to 350°F/180°C. Grease a 20-cm loose-bottomed quiche or tart pan.

Combine ¼ cup of sweetener, almond meal, coconut flour, cinnamon and butter. Spread mixture on the base of the tin only. Bake for 10 minutes.

For cheesecake filling, beat the cream cheese, the balance of the sweetener and vanilla in a large mixing bowl until light and fluffy. Add lime juice and eggs slowly into mixture while making sure to stir well.

Pour mixture over the pre-baked crust. Bake again for about 30 minutes. Cool on a wire rack. Cover and chill for at least 2 hours. Decorate with fresh lime zest just ahead of serving.

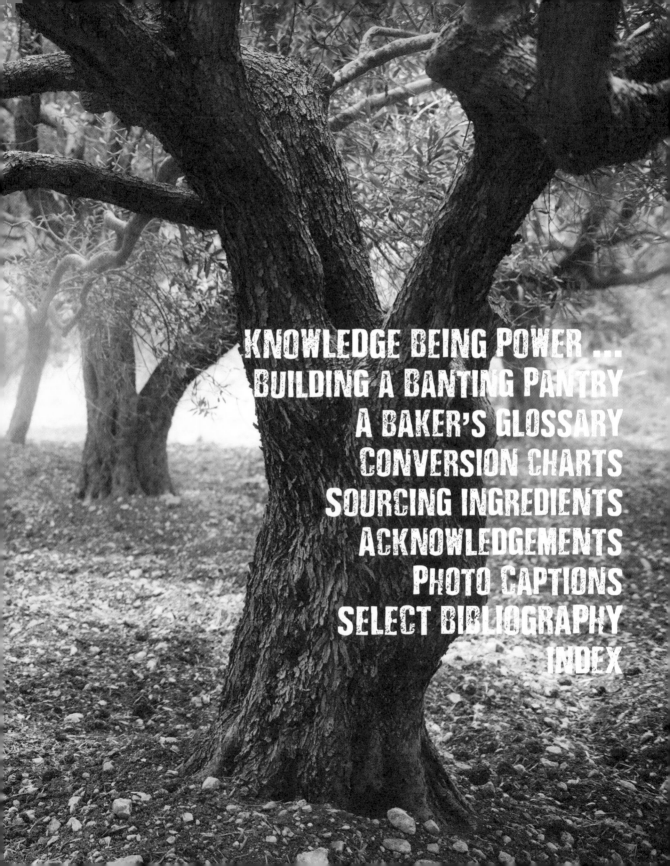

KNOWLEDGE BEING POWER ...

There are a couple of underlying principles, issues and terms that are so integral to this low-carb high-fat landscape and current thinking on optimal nutrition that it seems worthwhile to review some of these in more detail. There are also so many acronyms, so much terminology floating around, and often loads of conflicting information, that an understanding of some of the basic physiological and nutritional issues helps give you some perspective and possibly helps you make more informed choices. Feel free to skip right over it if it's stuff you're well acquainted with!

Anti-nutrients

These are natural or synthetic compounds found in a variety of foods, but in particular grains, legumes and nuts, that interfere with the absorption of vitamins, minerals and other nutrients by binding to them. They also inhibit certain digestive enzymes, which are vital for proper absorption. Phytic acid, leptins and saponins (see more info under Grains and Phytic Acid below) are examples of anti-nutrients. Foods rich in Vitamin C, like leafy green vegetables or citrus fruits, can, however, counteract phytate and increase iron absorption.

Antioxidants

Antioxidants are chemical substances that help protect against cell damage from free radicals. Free radicals are unstable, electron-deficient molecules that react with other molecules to gain electrons, causing oxidative damage to DNA which in turn contributes to ageing and the development of cancer. Well-known antioxidants include Vitamin A, Vitamin C, Vitamin E, carotenoids and flavonoids.

Antioxidants also increase HDL ('good') cholesterol levels and reduce LDL ('bad') cholesterol levels. This is partly due to increasing levels of Apo A-1 protein which clears cholesterol from blood vessels. Oxidation of LDL cholesterol causes it to enter the endothelial layer of blood vessels where it activates the endothelial cells and cells of the immune system to initiate inflammation. This ultimately forms inflamed and unstable 'plaques' which bulge into the arteries and block blood flow, or rupture and cause blood clotting, stroke or heart attack. Therefore, by preventing LDL cholesterol oxidation, antioxidants reduce the risk of atherosclerosis and cardiac arrest.

Antioxidant activity is measured as an Oxygen Radical Absorbance Capacity (ORAC) score. Foods with higher ORAC values have more antioxidant potential. ORAC values are almost never part of the nutritional data on labels though! See more info below under ORAC.

Body Mass Index (BMI)

Body Mass Index is a standardised ratio of weight to height, and is often used as a general indicator of health. Your BMI can be calculated by dividing your weight (in kilograms) by the square of your height (in metres). A BMI between 18.5 and 24.9 is considered normal for most adults, with anything higher usually an indication that an individual is overweight.

Calories

A calorie is a unit of measurement for energy. Weirdly enough, one calorie is formally defined as the amount of energy required to raise one cubic centimetre of water by one degree centigrade. For the purpose of measuring the amount of energy in food, nutritionists most commonly use kilocalories (equal to 1 000 calories), and label the measurement either as 'kcal' or as 'Calories' with a capital 'C'. One kcal is also equivalent to approximately 4.184 kilojoules. All calories are not created equal though – find more on this in the Low Carb Logic section.

Cholesterol

Cholesterol is a soft, waxy substance present in all parts of the body including the nervous system, skin, muscles, liver, intestines and heart. It is both made by the body and obtained from animal products in the diet. Cholesterol is manufactured in the liver for normal body functions, including the production of hormones, bile acid, and Vitamin D. It then enters the bloodstream where it combines with fatty acids to form high-density (HDL) and low-density (LDL) lipoproteins. LDLs are considered the 'bad cholesterol', since they can stick together to form plaque deposits on the walls of your blood vessels, leading to atherosclerosis.

For over 50 years, cholesterol has been considered the culprit behind rising rates of heart disease. New research, however, shows that there is little evidence that cholesterol is a cause of atherosclerosis, heart disease or stroke. On the contrary, there is now growing evidence available suggesting that cholesterol *protects* us from atherosclerosis, heart disease and stroke.

Cortisol

Cortisol is a hormone released in response to stress, activating our fight-or-flight mechanisms, and also functions in the management of inflammation. While critical to our survival, if stress levels become chronic and cortisol remains constantly elevated, insulin resistance and its corollary, fat storage, can occur – like a domino, cortisol sets off a release of glucose from your tissues to provide the energy needed for this fight/flight situation, and of course with the rise in glucose comes a rise in insulin, which signals the body to store fat. To add insult to injury, the body directs fat storage in the abdomen, around the organs, where there are more receptors for cortisol and a greater supply of blood.

Belly fat accumulation aside, the constant release of cortisol can eventually cause major functions in the body to shut down or operate sub-optimally, impacting in particular the immune function and digestion, and compromising memory function as well as the balance of dopamine and serotonin critical for psychological wellbeing. So make sure you find ways to let that steam out of the pot and be sure to get enough sleep, as lack of sleep also raises cortisol levels.

Dietary fibre

Dietary fibre comes from the thick cell walls of plants which, while edible, cannot be digested or absorbed in the small intestine and thus passes into the large intestine intact.

Fibre comes in two forms – soluble, which attracts water and then dissolves into a gluey mass, slowing down digestion, evening out blood sugar levels and trapping fats and sugars, bacteria and toxins which can then move out of the body; and insoluble, which actually speeds up the time it takes for material to move through the digestive tract, bulking your stools and 'scrubbing' the digestive tract lining, removing mucoid plaque, trapped toxins and other noxious materials.

While stimulation of digestion, prevention of constipation and the improving of blood glucose levels and blood lipid profiles are the primary benefits of a diet high in dietary fibre, other benefits are worth noting. Because fibre provides bulk in the diet, without added calories, it can have a satiating effect on appetite, helping in weight management.

In low-carb cooking, we add flax meal, chia meal and psyllium husk, for example, to baked goods not just because they provide some bulk and help to bind in the absence of gluten, but also because they add the roughage element your Gran always insisted you needed!

Essential amino acids

There are hundreds of amino acids in nature but there are only 20-odd biologically active amino acids at play in humans. Amino acids are the building blocks of protein, forming an almost endless variety of different proteins as they combine in different sequences. The origin of the word protein is from the Greek *protos*, meaning 'first', which interestingly reflects protein's critical value in human nutrition.

Nine of the amino acids in human biology are called 'essential' amino acids because they are amino acids that your body does not have the ability to synthesise and they must therefore be supplied by your diet. The nine essential amino acids are: histidine, isoleucine, leucine, lysine, methionine, phenylalanine, threonine, tryptophan and valine. In contrast, non-essential amino acids are those that can be produced from other amino acids and substances in the diet and through various metabolic processes.

There is a scoring system that articulates the amount of each essential amino acid that should be supplied per gram of protein – a score of 100 or above indicates a complete or high-quality protein; a score below 100 indicates a lower-quality protein. To be considered 'complete', a protein must contain all nine of the essential amino acids in roughly equal amounts. So by this system, meat and eggs are complete proteins, and beans and nuts aren't.

The amount of protein each of us needs will vary depending on a number of factors, including activity levels, age, muscle mass, physique goals and current state of health. The current Recommended Dietary Allowance (RDA) for protein is a mere 0.8 grams of protein per kilogram of body weight. This is generally considered a bare minimum though, with levels of up to 30% of daily caloric intake suggested to be from proteins. Be aware though that the roughly 1 gram of protein per kilogram of body weight refers to the nett protein content – a 230 g serving of beef only contains 61 grams of actual protein and a large egg weighs around 55-odd grams, but it only contains about 6 grams of protein.

Fats and essential fatty acids

The terms 'fats' and 'fatty acids' are often used interchangeably in lay literature and by the media. In fact, fatty acids are sub-units of fats. Most of the common fats that we eat and the fat we store in our body are triglycerides, or more technically acylglycerols, which are fatty acids (the acyl group) linked to an alcohol (glycerol) via an ester bond. Fatty acids are also incorporated in all cell membranes as compounds called phospholipids, and when fats are broken down (the ester bond is cleaved) and taken out of the fat cells and transported in the bloodstream, they are then known as free fatty acids. Chemically speaking, fatty acids consist of a chain of carbon atoms, with a methyl group at one end and an acid group at the other. Each carbon atom has a number of hydrogen atoms attached to it – the exact number of hydrogen atoms on each carbon then determines whether the fat is saturated or unsaturated.

So saturated fatty acids (SFAs) contain the maximum level of hydrogen atoms possible, while in unsaturated fatty acids, some of the hydrogen atoms are missing and have been replaced with double bonds between the carbon atoms. Saturated fats are usually solid at room temperature – examples of foods with a high percentage of saturated fats include butter, coconut oil, palm kernel oil and lard.

Unsaturated fats are usually liquid at room temperature. A fat is termed 'monounsaturated' (MUFAs) if there is one double bond, and 'polyunsaturated' (PUFAs) if there are two or more double bonds. Examples of fats with high percentages of monounsaturated fats are olive oil, avo oil and mustard oil, and the marrow of bones, which is why bone broth is valued in the low-carb diet, whereas PUFAs tend to be found in seed oils, such as soy, corn, sunflower and safflower oil.

Excess consumption of polyunsaturated oils has been shown to contribute to a large number of disease conditions including increased cancer and heart disease; immune system dysfunction; damage to the liver, reproductive organs and lungs; digestive disorders; depressed learning ability; impaired growth; and weight gain. PUFAs, already unstable chemically, are rendered even more so by virtue of the industrial extraction processes now in play, which generate high levels of heat and exposure to light and oxygen and chemicals. The carbon bonds are broken, thereby creating free radicals, which are highly reactive as they go 'scavenging' around the body, looking for 'completion' and in so doing attack cell membranes and red blood cells and causing damage in DNA/RNA strands, and thus triggering mutations in tissue, blood vessels and skin.

So while we need to stay aware of our overall or absolute levels of PUFA intake, there is also much interest in medical, health and nutritional circles about the relativity of our omega-6 vs omega-3 fatty acid levels, which are the two sub groups we find in PUFAs. Alpha linolenic acid (ALA) is the so-called 'parent' fatty acid for the omega-3 family of fatty acids because the liver can make other omega-3 fatty acids from it. DHA (docosahexaenoic acid) and EPA (eicosapentaenoic acid) are in fact the preferred sources of omega-3s, and while the body can produce these from ALA, the conversion is not optimal which is why obtaining DHA and EPA directly from the diet is advised. Similarly, linoleic acid (LA) is the 'parent' fatty acid for the synthesis of other omega-6 fatty acids in the liver.

There is significant data showing that over the last 150 years, intake of omega-6 has increased and intake of omega-3 has decreased in parallel with the increase in heart disease. In hunter-gatherer societies, the ratio of omega-6 to omega-3 in the diet is around 2:1; however, the endless increase in the use of vegetable and seed oils in the processed foods consumed in urban society has raised that ratio to as high as 20:1. Too much omega-6 in the diet creates an imbalance that can interfere with production of important prostaglandins. This disruption can result in increased tendency to form blood clots, inflammation, high blood pressure, irritation of the digestive tract, depressed immune function, sterility, cell proliferation, cancer and weight gain.

The prevailing current recommendation to improve the omega-6 to omega-3 ratio is to increase the amount of omega-3 fatty acids in the diet, while reducing the amount of omega-6. In the low-carb universe, omega-6 fatty acids are naturally reduced by virtue of the exclusion of polyunsaturated oils. Good sources of omega-3 fatty acids include the oils in fatty fish such as salmon or sardines, and walnuts and chia seed.

The technicalities of biochemistry aside, dietary

fats and oils are the most concentrated form of energy we can take in as they yield 9 calories/g, whereas carbohydrates and proteins yield only 4 calories/g.

Glycaemic index and load

As we know, when carbohydrates are digested, glucose is released into the bloodstream. The glycaemic index is a comparative measurement of the amount of glucose released by a particular food over a two- to three-hour period. Glucose itself is the benchmark, with a rating of 100.

Foods that rapidly release glucose rate high on the glycaemic index (GI). Foods that slowly release glucose are low on the glycaemic index. Low glycaemic index foods are absorbed more slowly, so they stay in your digestive tract longer. This is why these foods are sometimes called 'slow carbs'. A low GI score is generally considered to be one that is 55 or less, with a medium GI sitting at between 56 and 69, and a high GI running at 70 or more.

Clearly the GI rating alone does not give you all the information you need to determine a food's effect on your blood sugar. It only tells you how quickly the carbs in a food should turn into sugar in your blood. The glycaemic load or GL is a more accurate form of analysis as it tells you how much of that carb the food contains. Essentially, the GL is equal to the glycaemic index of a food multiplied by the number of grams of carbohydrates in the serving of food that's being eaten as obviously the amount you eat of that particular food is also a huge factor in the rise of your blood sugar. A GL of above 20 is considered high, the 11–19 range is considered average, and below 11 is low.

It is important to remember that the GI scale is simply a comparative scale; it compares one food's blood glucose response to another. As is obvious, there are many other factors to consider when choosing your food.

Grains

So what is so bad about grains (and legumes for that matter) that they're off the Banting good-to-go list?

One of the reasons we struggle to digest grains and legumes is because they contain lectins, which are a class of proteins found in many types of seeds (like wheat, oats, barley, rice, peanuts, soy, etc.) and are part of the plant's natural defence mechanism. As a digested seed cannot grow into a new plant, Nature developed ways to deter us from eating them by making us sick or resisting digestion completely or both. Since the agricultural revolution about 9 000 odd years ago, we've managed to domesticate them and incorporate them in our diets, but that is a very recent and short time period in human history, and our genes haven't adapted fully to their consumption.

Lectins are not fully compatible with our digestive enzymes, and also contain protease inhibitors with the result that they pass through the digestive tract largely intact, doing damage to the cells that line the tract along the way, so that microscopic holes open up. This is otherwise known as leaky-gut syndrome. Once there is a breach in the wall, so to speak, lectins and other toxins 'leak out' into the bloodstream, attaching to any tissue they can, and stimulating an antibody response which destroys both the invader and the invaded unfortunately. Apart from the possibility of the development of an autoimmune disorder as a result, at best leaky-gut syndrome results in impaired absorption of nutrients from the digestive tract, changes in the composition of the gut flora, i.e. the balance between the good guys and the bad guys, and high levels of inflammation, with energy that could be used for tissue repair now going into damage control.

Gluten is a lectin and possibly the most damaging one, because parts of it closely resemble some of the proteins in our bodies, and when the body responds to the presence of gluten that has escaped the gut, it forms antibodies which do not distinguish between the human and 'alien' proteins and can thus also target the body's own cells. Lectins also cause leptin resistance, which means that your hunger signal is suppressed and that you'll be hungry even when your body has had more than enough calories (see below). Dairy and the nightshade veggies also contain lectins by the way, which might explain why some people battle to digest these.

Legumes, and pseudo-grains, like amaranth for example, then also contain very high doses of saponins, which are also defence mechanisms inherent in certain plants, that have the ability to interact with the cholesterol molecules imbedded in the surface membrane of every cell in the body and to rearrange those cholesterol molecules to form a stable, pore-like complex, thus also increasing the permeability of the gut.

In the past, these anti-nutrients were intuitively understood and mitigated by soaking and fermenting the foods containing them and grinding the whole kernels only when they were just about to be used. Now, however, we no longer observe these practices. The inherent biochemical issues with grains (and other high-lectin foods) are aggravated by the fact that we have now created genetically modified, 'high-yield', high-gluten-content grains which are grown with huge synthetic chemical inputs and then bleached and processed by industrial steel-roller mills, stripping much of the nutrient content in the process.

Proteins, vitamins, lipids and minerals found in the bran and germ are lost when the whole grains are turned into a flour which is designed to last pretty much indefinitely and be shipped over long distances to provide inexpensive sustenance for the masses.

Leptin and ghrelin

Metabolism, appetite, satiety and other factors influence body weight through a complex interplay of various hormones, including leptin, which is an appetite-suppressant hormone produced in the fat cells that plays a key role in the body's metabolism. Leptin tells your brain when you've had enough to eat and your stomach is full. However, as you can become insulin resistant, so you can become leptin resistant. Leptin resistance makes you 'satiety-resistant', meaning your brain doesn't get the message to say it's okay to stop eating now. A vicious cycle kicks in as the more body fat you have, the more leptin you produce and the more the receptors then ignore/become resistant/lose their sensitivity to the signals.

Ghrelin, on the other hand, is regarded as a hormone that increases appetite. It is released primarily in the stomach and is thought to signal hunger to the brain, telling us when we really need a nutrient intake and thus rising before meals and then falling after meals. It is believed that fasting can help normalise ghrelin levels so that it actually becomes more accurate in telling you if you really do need to eat or not. Too much ghrelin is likely to make you eat more, just as too little leptin means you won't know when to stop.

When people are subjected to sleep loss, leptin levels fall and ghrelin levels rise. In a joint study conducted by Stanford University and the University of Wisconsin that measured leptin and ghrelin levels, body fat and sleep amounts in 1 000 people, the participants that slept the fewest hours a night weighed the most. So get that sleep time banked!

Nutrient density

Nutrient density is the measurement of the amount of a nutrient per fixed portion of food. It is one of the main satiety triggers – if your food is nutrient poor, your stomach may become full, but you're left starving at the cellular level and you're likely to overeat, whereas nutrient-rich foods help you to feel full, while delivering a whole host of other functional attributes that assist your body to attain better health. By nutrient rich we really mean foods with higher levels of nourishment for growth or metabolism including factors such as essential fatty acids, proteins, vitamins and minerals.

ORAC

ORAC stands for Oxygen Radical Absorbance Capacity. It is essentially a database of antioxidant levels compiled by scientists at the National Institutes of Health in the US. The ORAC method isn't the final say on antioxidant measurement, as for one, the ORAC value of a particular food can vary significantly depending on whether the food is measured based on units per gram dry weight or units per gram wet weight – think grapes versus raisins for example. It is useful though as a measure of relative values.

Organic

The word 'organic' refers to the way farmers grow and process agricultural products, such as fruit, vegetables, grains, dairy products and meat. Organic farming practices are designed to encourage soil and water conservation and reduce pollution and therefore go beyond human concerns to address the broader environment we exist in.

And while the jury is out as to whether organically and conventionally produced foodstuffs are significantly different in their nutrient content, it's what's *not* in the organically grown food and what's missing from the conventionally produced stuff that is worth considering, as well as the bigger picture of the effects our industrialised farming practices have on the earth, the growing need to support small local businesses and the impact on the other species we share this blue dot with.

Conventional, commercial agriculture has massively depleted most soils of beneficial minerals as herbicides like glyphosate act as chelators, effectively blocking the uptake and utilisation of minerals. These sprays are furthermore composed of powerful chemicals like organophosphorus, which can leave a residue on produce and which has been connected to a number of developmental problems, including autism and ADHD. It stands to reason that not having pesticides, chemicals or processed additives bogging down your system means a smaller risk of disease, illness and disorders.

Yes, organic foods typically cost more than their conventional counterparts. Much of the higher cost is due to the smaller scale of production given the lower demand and also to the fact that it is a more labour-intensive process. Arguably, the more people begin to make this choice, the greater the economies of scale that should arise as more farmers are encouraged to assume these farming practices, which would ultimately result in more organic options at better prices.

That said, recent research suggests that choosing organic food can lead to increased intake of nutritionally desirable antioxidants and reduced exposure to toxic heavy metals. So even if they look less than perfect (courtesy of the absence of waxes and preservatives), at least you'll know that they are free of irradiation and genetic modification, and truly fresh as organic foods tend to be seasonal.

Phytic acid

Nuts, seeds and legumes store phosphorus as phytic acid in the outer or bran layer, as well as enzyme inhibitors to prevent them from sprouting when conditions are not suitable. This is Nature's brilliant way of preserving genetic plant material until it has a viable chance of producing a plant. For humans, though, phytic acid is often considered an anti-nutrient because it binds minerals in the digestive tract, making them less available to our bodies.

Phytic acid not only grabs onto or chelates important minerals, but also inhibits enzymes that we need to digest our food. In the LCHF paradigm we use loads of nuts and seeds, so we're presented with something of a challenge then in terms of their phytic acid content. Soaking, fermenting and sprouting all replicate germination, convincing the seeds that it's time to begin their growth processes. Germination, which activates and multiplies nutrients (particularly vitamins A, B and C), neutralises enzyme inhibitors, and promotes the growth of vital digestive enzymes including phytase, which neutralises the phytic acid). See more on treating nuts and seeds ahead of consumption in the Building Blocks section.

Satiation and satiety

Hunger is an internal mechanism which helps ensure that we consume enough energy for our needs. As we all know, the less we eat or the longer we're not able to eat, the hungrier we become, and the longer it takes for hunger to subside once we do begin to eat.

Satiation refers to the point at which we've had enough during a meal while satiety refers to the feeling of satisfaction or 'fullness' after the consumption of food. This feeling of fullness can play an important role in controlling how much we eat – if we feel satiated after a meal, we can run longer before the next meal, and might even eat less at it.

While many things are known to influence satiety – including individual differences in endocrinal-system functioning – one of the biggest factors is the type of food that we eat. Some foods fill our stomachs faster and/or remain in our stomachs longer, and therefore do a better job of holding off hunger. The 'Fullness Factor' is a term that has been coined by NutritionData to express how filling a food might be per calorie. Interestingly, on their list, sucrose and glucose rate really low.

In low-carb high-fat thinking, the fact that fat contains more calories per gram than either protein or carb-oriented foods suggests that the energy release is more sustained, providing better satiety over a longer period or, simply put, fat is filling. Carbs are broken down faster than either proteins or fats. That said, as noted already, fibre has an important role to play in the satiety equation, so making sure that you incorporate fibre along with some protein in each meal is likely to keep you going for longer.

BUILDING A BANTING PANTRY

You've got to hack your pantry. Brutal and radical as this might seem, keeping the no-no stuff around is asking for temptation or habit to block you on your way to your new you. And once the 'substitute' ingredients are in place, you'll find that creating foods that are delicious and satisfying (even if they seem slightly strange versions of old favourites like pizza) does not require a degree in rocket science or the employment of a full-time personal chef.

If you treat it as an adventure into new territory, it can go way beyond the kitchen and the functional requirement of keeping your machine running. Preparing different food can become a way to explore the city you live in more thoroughly, as you hunt for outlets of the ingredients you want, a way to 'play' with friends and family and an avenue for your own gastronomic creativity, as you combine flavours and ingredients you've not worked with much before.

If you're unsure you're going to like something, buy a small quantity first, and then if it makes your taste buds sing, you can look for bulk options that should bring costs down a little.

A note on which …

Eating this way is costly in terms of what you pay for the base ingredients. The equation is a complex one though, as the nutritional density of these foods is also high, which means a little goes a long way for the most part. And arguably the health benefits that will undoubtedly arise have a value too. In fact, some would call these priceless.

You may also find that you 'eat in' more, as you prepare more meals in your own kitchen, which brings about a whole bunch of other dynamics that you might find of value!

Getting back to the clearing out, it's pretty obvious what has to go if you're going to observe a low-carb high-fat diet:

• Grain-based foods

• Tinned goods high is sugar and preservatives

• ALL the polyunsaturated veg/seed oils

• High GL fruits and veg (if not entirely, then to be savoured only in small amounts)

• Most 'lite' versions of anything – yoghurt/salad dressing, etc.

The above 'lite designation' tends to refer to fat content rather than sugar content, and flavour that is lost stripping out the fats is replaced with sweeteners and other kinds of artificial flavourings.

As a rule of thumb, you want as little from the grocery store as possible around you, with as much from the greengrocer and a trustworthy butcher instead.

When you do buy packaged goods, READ THE LABEL – anything that sounds like it was concocted by a scientist rather than Mother Nature is likely to be something your body finds alien and should thus logically be avoided.

There are certain foods that you really want to incorporate as much as possible, due to their high nutritional density, their fat content, and their capacity to add fantastic flavour, to mention just a few of their qualities. Below is some information on some of the ingredients that are particular to, and possibly most important in, a low-carb pantry.

Animal proteins

Meat is among the best sources of protein, being rich in healthy fatty acids, vitamins and minerals. It is a particularly good source of creatine, carnosine and carnitine, as well as other unique nutrients that cannot be derived from plants.

If you can, it is by far the best to eat meat from animals that have been raised in natural environments, and with their natural foods, such as grass-fed beef. Cows are ruminants and their digestive systems are developed to eat grass. Pasture-raised animals enjoy a much higher quality of life than those confined within industrialised 'factory farming' environments, moving around freely and eating the way ruminants are meant to eat. Grain-fed animals are usually crowded into cramped facilities, often without access to fresh air or sunlight with their unnatural diet causing all manner of health problems. Both their unnatural diets and the stressful, overcrowded conditions they are raised in are a breeding ground for bacteria, which is why they are routinely treated with antibiotics to prevent outbreaks of disease. Antibiotic resistance is a common outcome, which many are claiming has contributed to the development of the 'superbugs' that now affect humans. Add the synthetic growth hormones and/or steroids they're subjected to in order to speed up their growth, and you have a potent cocktail of misery and toxicity that you do not want to be taking on board.

And it's not just your own body that bears thinking about as industrial farming involves large amounts of fossil fuels to truck feed and animal waste around, and the use of herbicides and pesticides on crops grown for feed which pollute the air,

ground water and soil, all of which have a terribly disruptive effect on the environment. Interestingly, the European Union has banned the use of implants in beef and refuses to import American beef treated with chemicals even though trade sanctions have been levied against them for this action. If you are what you eat, you are what you eat ate. So while truly pasture-raised meat comes at a premium, it's worth considering the hidden personal and collective costs of the industrial system when you make your choice.

Numerous studies have shown that both the meat and the milk derived from grass-fed beef contains more omega-3 fatty acids, more CLA, more antioxidants, and more vitamins and minerals than that from grain-fed animals. The same applies to other forms of red meat (including wild meats or venison) and poultry, so even though you might have to work a little harder to find it, the health benefits alone are worth the effort. Beware you don't allow yourself to be 'greenwashed' by labels containing terms that actually don't mean much as there are loads of suppliers out there who will happily have you thinking that their animals were raised ethically, when in fact they actually weren't. For example, 'pasture-raised' doesn't always mean livestock has grass to eat, and 'access to the outdoors' can mean only a small doorway in one side of a densely packed barn – see note on free-range eggs below!

In addition to grass-fed red meats and naturally fed poultry, the so called 'fatty' fish such as salmon are also very rich in high-quality proteins and many nutrients. Most of the fats are omega-3 fatty acids, which most us don't get enough of. The big BUT here is that while we might think that fish are caught as they freely roam the seas and rivers, most of the salmon in supermarkets has been farmed, so you're looking at the same level of antibiotic and other noxious content.

The Environmental Working Group, working with other researchers in Canada, Ireland and the UK, have found that cancer-causing polychlorinated biphenyls (PCBs) exist in farm-raised salmon at 16 times the rate of wild salmon. So look out for wild-caught salmon or at least wild-farmed, RSPCA-approved salmon, as this way you'll know it's clean.

Cacao/cocoa

Botanically, cacao is a nut, with the chocolate most of us are at least somewhat enslaved to coming from cacao beans, which are in turn the seeds of the cacao fruit. Rich in magnesium (the highest source of magnesium in all foods in fact) and flavonol antioxidants, cacao contains far more antioxidants per 100 g than acai berries, goji berries or blueberries.

It is also a great source of serotonin, dopamine and phenylethylamine, three well-studied neurotransmitters, as well as the amino acid tryptophan, all of which help alleviate depression and are associated with feelings of wellbeing – little wonder it's the go-to substance for many of us when stuff goes down that exceeds our stress thresholds. It's the trash that goes into commercial chocolate that puts it on the 'to be seriously avoided' list.

However, using raw cacao nibs, powder and butter are perfectly permissible, if not downright desirable, given the properties noted above. Blend the nibs into your smoothies (great with a shot of organic espresso), or add to your trail mixes and granolas. Use the powder and butter for raw desserts and treats. Expensive they most certainly are, but with an intensity of flavour that results in a little giving a lot of satisfaction.

So, what's the difference between raw cacao and cocoa powder? Both are produced by grinding cocoa nibs to a paste or liquor and then removing the cocoa butter (the fat component of the cocoa).

During the production of raw cacao powder, the cocoa butter is removed by cold-pressing, with the temperature constantly monitored to ensure it does not exceed about 40°C – in theory at any rate, given there is no certifying body monitoring this.

Cocoa powder, on the other hand, arises from a process where the beans are hydraulically pressed to remove the cocoa butter, and this process generates lots of heat, frequently in excess of 150°C. Look out for natural, unsweetened cocoa powder if you can find it, which is bitter and slightly acidic, and needs to be paired with an alkali, such as baking soda, to reduce the acidity. Most commercial cocoa powder, however, is Dutch processed, which means it has its natural acids neutralised with an alkali, but this results in it having up to 90% fewer antioxidants than natural cocoa powder. It is less bitter though, with a milder, mellower flavour. As heat destroys the antioxidants, it makes sense to use raw cacao for raw dishes and natural, unsweetened cocoa for baked goods.

Cocoa butter is great to use when making your own raw chocolate, although you can substitute it with coconut oil or butter in some instances, which is less costly.

Chocolate

This favourite and familiar food and ingredient gets its name from xocolatl, an Aztec word that means 'bitter water'. Many forms of chocolate are used in the culinary arena, but whether it is unsweetened, milk, bittersweet or semi-sweet chocolate, all of these forms use a base of 'cocoa liquor' that is derived from ground, roasted and blended small pieces of the cacao bean nibs. The higher the cocoa percentage, the lower the percentage of other ingredients, such as milk solids or sugar, which is why the highest cocoa percentage you can handle is recommended when you're desperate for a little fix – dark chocolate has an ORAC score of 21 000 by the way, an indication of the level of antioxidants it contains. Truly medicinal stuff!

Coconut

Is a coconut a fruit, nut or seed? Tricky question, depending on how you look at it, as in fact it qualifies as all three. In the most technical botanical sense though, a coconut is a one-seeded drupe, or a 'dry drupe'. Drupes are a subset of fruits, with a hard stony covering enclosing the seed and a fleshy outer layer (like cherries, olives and many culinary nuts). The nutrients and physical characteristics change as a coconut matures – young coconuts have more 'water' and soft, gel-like flesh, and mature coconuts have less 'water' and firm flesh.

Given that every bit of the coconut can be used, it is little wonder that coconut palms are called the 'tree of life' in many cultures, as they can produce a beverage, fibre, food, fuel, utensils, musical instruments and much more. On a dietary and culinary level alone, the coconut is arguably deserving of the title 'superfood', given its nutritional profile and the fact that we can use the coconut flesh (fresh or dried), the water, the milk or cream, the fat or oil, and the sweetener that is derived from the coconut blossom nectar. In fact, coconut is an indispensable food item for most people under the tropical belt. It is a complete food rich in calories, vitamins and minerals. A medium-sized nut, carrying 400 g edible flesh and some 30–150 ml of water, may provide almost all the daily-required essential minerals, vitamins and energy for an average-sized individual.

Although its flesh is disproportionately high in saturated fats in comparison to other common edible nuts, coconut has many bioactive compounds that are essential for better health. And the important saturated fatty acid in the coconut is lauric acid. Lauric acid increases good-HDL cholesterol levels in the blood (HDL is high-density lipoprotein, which has beneficial effects on the coronary arteries by preventing vessel blockade aka atherosclerosis).

Coconut cream is made from pressing the coconut flesh. Coconut milk is made from the expressed juice of grated coconut flesh and water. Coconut water, on the other hand, is actually the juice present inside the interior cavity or endosperm of young, tender coconuts. Its water is one of nature's most refreshing drinks, consumed worldwide for its nutritious and health-benefiting properties, composed as it is of a very particular combination of sugars, B-complex vitamins such as riboflavin, niacin, thiamine and pyridoxine, and folates, minerals, enzymes, amino acids, cytokine and phyto-hormones. Fresh coconut juice is also one of the highest sources of electrolytes known to humankind, and can be used to prevent dehydration, for instance in cases of diarrhoea or strenuous exercise, instead of a sugary sports drink.

Desiccated coconut is unsweetened, very finely ground coconut with most of the moisture removed. Unlike coconut flour, which has the fat removed, desiccated coconut retains all the saturated fatty-acid goodness. Flaked coconut, meanwhile, is pretty much the same animal, just in flatter, wider pieces.

Coconut flour is made from ground and dried coconut flesh. One of the many health benefits of coconut flour is its high levels of healthy saturated fats in the form of medium-chain fatty acids (MCFA). These are used by the body easily for energy and help to support a healthy metabolism, and balanced blood sugar levels. It is also high in fibre and protein, and low in sugar, digestible carbohydrates and calories, with a low score on the glycaemic index. See more in the Flours section below.

Coconut oil is covered in the Fats section below.

Stock up your pantry with every available form of coconut you can find, and look out for fresh coconuts that show up in the greengrocer every now and then!

Dairy

Dairy products remain controversial, being praised by many health organisations as an essential food for bone health with other experts of the view that dairy is harmful and should be avoided. Before the agricultural revolution, humans only drank mother's milk as infants. They didn't consume dairy as adults, which is one of the reasons dairy is considered 'unnatural' and is excluded in many health regimens. About 75% of the world's population suffers from lactose intolerance as we lose the ability as we grow up to produce the digestive enzyme lactase, which breaks down lactose (the main form of carbohydrate in dairy).

It is, however, full of highly bioavailable saturated fat, protein and carbs in equal measure and for those who can tolerate it, there are numerous studies showing that dairy products have clear benefits for bone health, improving bone density in the young and lowering the risk of fractures in the elderly.

That said, of course, not all dairy products are the same, varying greatly depending on how the cows were raised and how the dairy was processed. Cows that are raised on pasture and fed grass have more omega-3 fatty acids and up to 500% more CLA. Grass-fed dairy is also much higher in fat-soluble vitamins, especially Vitamin K2, a nutrient that is incredibly important for regulating calcium metabolism and has major benefits for both bone and heart health. Keep in mind that these healthy fats and fat-soluble vitamins are not present in low-fat or skim dairy products, which are often loaded with sugar to make up for the lack of flavour caused by removing the fat.

Butter
See the Fats section below.

Buttermilk/amasi
Back in the good old days, buttermilk was a by-product of churning cream into butter, hence the name. Sadly, commercial buttermilk is often made from low-fat milk and a souring agent, so look out for full-fat versions.

Cheese
Cheese is among the richest dietary sources of calcium and an excellent source of the milk protein, casein, which is rich in essential amino acids and generally highly digestible. Fat content varies with the type of cheese, but is largely of the saturated form, with good levels of CLA (conjugated linoleic acid, an important essential fatty acid). Go for organic where you can get it and look out for hidden ingredients like thickening agents in goods like cream cheese and animal rennet in cheeses like grana padano or parmigiana.

Cream
Cream is an energy-dense food that comes in many forms, with the nutritional value varying accordingly, but those with a higher fat content have a richer texture and a more flavourful taste, and do not curdle easily when used in cooking. Higher fat creams also have a greater Vitamin A content than lower fat creams; while lower fat cream has a higher protein content. The quantity of butter fat in cream determines how easily it can be whipped, so pick your pony depending on what you're intending to use it for. As with all dairy, choose cream from pasture-reared cows not subjected to any unnatural hormonal stimulation where you can.

Milk
Milk adds moisture and nutritional value in baked goods. Full-cream milk contains between 3.5 and

4% butter fat and nearly 5% sugar in the form of lactose, so remember that when you order your third cappuccino.

A note on goat's milk – goat's milk is believed to be more easily digestible and less allergenic than cow's milk as structurally and nutritionally it is one of the closer corollaries to human breast milk. It contains around 10 grams of fat per 8 ounces (230 ml) compared to 8 to 9 grams in whole cow's milk, and unlike cow's milk, goat's milk does not contain agglutinin. As a result, the fat globules in goat's milk do not cluster together even when pasteurised, making them easier to digest.

Yoghurt
Produced when milk is fermented with acidophilus bacteria, full-fat yoghurt, with roughly 3.5% fat, tastes and behaves very differently from that emaciated low- or fat-free stuff, which is used in products then loaded with sugar in an attempt to put some kind of palatability back into it. If it is made the real way, yoghurt will contain beneficial bacteria and function as a probiotic, which aids the immune and digestive systems. Plain yoghurt made from whole milk contains about 8.5 grams of protein per cup, made up of both whey and casein.

Ultimately, as it is with most things in nutrition, the health effects of dairy depend on the individual – just make sure to choose quality full-fat dairy and watch how your body responds to it.

Eggs
Eggs are a veritable superfood, containing all the vitamins, minerals, protein and fatty acids that we need, and delivering a great sense of satiety however we eat them. One large (roughly 55/60 g) egg contains about 5 g of fat and 6 g of protein, containing all the essential amino acids (half of which is in the yolk by the way, so use whole eggs as much as possible) and is loaded with choline, Vitamin E, Vitamin A, Vitamin D, Vitamin K2,

omega-3 fats, iron and beta-carotene and other antioxidants.

In fact, eggs are one of the few foods considered to be a complete protein, because they contain all nine essential amino acids. Despite this nutritional punch, eggs were demonised for a long time, as their inherent cholesterol content was deemed to have a causative effect on our own blood cholesterol, which has now come to be reconsidered.

As with dairy, though, not all eggs are equal. Ethical considerations aside, chickens raised in stressful environments – eating corn and soy, pumped with antibiotics, and relegated to a tiny cage that would result in atrophy were it not for the steroids – do not produce high-quality eggs. When it comes to quality of life, there is no comparison between the life of truly free-range hens and that of battery-cage hens, and that quality of life shows up in the eggs. Eggs from hens that are truly free range and naturally fed (natural for chickens that is) have a much higher nutritional value and are specifically higher in omega-3s, beta-carotene and the vitamins E and A. One US study has also shown that free-range eggs are also 98% less likely to carry salmonella than those from chickens raised in battery cages.

However, be very aware that 'free range' is something of a loose term, with interpretations varying wildly, and not much by way of oversight in this country, so where you can, procure yourself eggs from somewhere you know the chickens really, really do run around freely and are fed their natural foods.

Wash the eggs just before cracking them so that you clean any bacteria on the shell that might contaminate the egg as you crack it. Oddly, some recipes talk about a volume of eggs, such as half a cup, so as a rule of thumb, you need 4 extra large, 5 large or 6 medium eggs to deliver a cup's worth.

Eggs are also easier to separate when they're cold, as in straight from the fridge.

Fats

Given this is a book on low-carb high-fat eating, it seems worth spending a little time looking at the fats we're going to dump and those we're going to include in our new pantries!

Trying to find the healthiest oil to cook with is something of a daunting task. Particularly when you're cooking at a high heat, you want to use oils that are stable and don't oxidise or go rancid easily. When oils undergo oxidation, they react with oxygen to form free radicals and other harmful compounds that you definitely don't want to be taking on board.

An important factor in determining an oil's resistance to oxidation and rancidification, both at high and low heat, is the relative degree of saturation of the fatty acids in it. Saturated fats have only single bonds in the fatty acid molecules, monounsaturated fats have one double bond, and polyunsaturated fats have two or more. It is these double bonds that are chemically reactive and sensitive to heat. Saturated fats and monounsaturated fats are thus more resistant to heating, but oils that are high in polyunsaturated fats should be avoided for cooking.

Knowing the smoke point of an oil is important because heating oil to the point where it begins to smoke continuously is the very same moment in time when its fat molecules start to break down at a much faster rate, producing toxic fumes and harmful free radicals. The refining process, which removes impurities along with nutrients from oil, raises the smoke point and prolongs shelf life, but the flip side is that it brings with it a bucket load of chemicals, so try to stick with organic, unrefined, cold-processed oils. Avoid oils that are high in

polyunsaturated fats (such as corn, cottonseed, soy, sunflower and certain other seed oils) as they're also loaded with omega-6s and most of us have too many of these in our diets anyway.

However, the truth is that sometimes you'll want that wok or skillet ripping hot. So for those rare occasions when you indulge in high-temperature cooking, use oils with a higher smoke point, such as hazelnut oil, high oleic sunflower oil (84% monounsaturated), avo oil or ghee (clarified butter).

For low-temperature cooking, or for dressing dishes and salad dressings, chose oils with higher levels of omega-3 fatty acids as they promote healthy cells, decrease stroke and heart attack risk and have an anti-inflammatory action.

While you need to pay attention to the smoke point, you also need to look at the ratio of omega-3 to omega-6 and even omega-9 fatty acids (omega-6s are pro-inflammatory, while omega-3s have an anti-inflammatory effect). In traditional and historical hunter-gatherer cultures on a non-industrial diet we see omega-6: omega-3 ratios of about 4:1 to 1:4, with most being somewhere in between. The ratio in today's Western diet is more like 16:1, much higher than what we are genetically adapted to.

Animal fats – lard, tallow, bacon drippings

The fatty acid content of animals tends to vary depending on what the animals eat. If they are fed on grains, the fats will contain quite a bit of polyunsaturated fats. If the animals are pasture raised or grass fed, there will be more saturated and monounsaturated fats in them. Ethical considerations aside once again, it makes complete sense to buy products that are from animals that were raised free of chemicals and on their natural diets.

Avo oil

Its fatty-acid profile is similar to that of olive oil, but it has an even higher smoke point, making it a decent choice for cooking. As with olive oil, buy in dark green glass bottles to minimise oxidation.

Butter

With its 68% saturated, 28% monounsaturated and lowly 4% polyunsaturated fat content, this most delightful substance has been much maligned in the past, whereas it is its manmade counterpart, margarine, that is the really evil stuff. We now know that saturated fats raise HDL (the 'good') cholesterol and change the LDL from small, dense (very bad) to large LDL, which is benign. Additionally, butter contains a decent amount of short- and medium-chain fats, which are metabolised differently from other fats and lead to improved satiety and increased fat burning.

Apart from its fat profile, butter is rich in fat-soluble vitamins, including vitamins A, E and K_2. Vitamin K_2 can have powerful effects on health as it is intimately involved in calcium metabolism and a low intake has been associated with many serious diseases, including cardiovascular disease, cancer and osteoporosis. Again, dairy from grass-fed cows is particularly rich in Vitamin K_2, so try to find butter derived from grass-fed, hormone-free cows so that it is as close to the state it would have been when your great-grandparents made their own down on the farm.

Using clarified butter or ghee strips out the milk sugars that can result in butter burning at higher temperatures, while retaining the quotient of vitamins A, E and K_2 as well as the fatty acids, conjugated linoleic acid (or CLA, a fatty acid which has powerful effects on metabolism and is actually sold commercially as a weight loss supplement) and butyrate, which is anti-inflammatory and has powerful protective effects on the digestive system. To prepare your own clarified butter, melt butter very gently in a saucepan and then bring it to the boil. Ladle the clear butter through a muslin-lined sieve, leaving the milky deposit behind.

Coconut oil

Most dietary fat is made of molecules called long-chain triglycerides (LCTs). As a 92% saturated fat, coconut oil contains loads of lauric acid, which is a type of medium-chain triglyceride (or MCT – see below for more) that is incredibly heat stable. Lauric acid increases the good HDL cholesterol in the blood to help *improve* cholesterol ratio levels. Coconut oil is also relatively low in omega-6 and is also a rich source of capric and caprylic acid, which with lauric acid work together to offer us antioxidant, anti-fungal and antibacterial properties.

Coconut butter is to coconut oil as butter is to ghee, being made from whole coconut flesh, with all the delicious fat *and* the solids included. It spreads well and by virtue of the coconut flesh content it has a natural sweetness that is just delicious.

Flax oil

Flax oil contains lots of the plant form of electron-rich, unsaturated fatty acids, and in particular the omega-3 alpha linolenic acid (ALA). You can use cold pressed flax oil as an omega-3 supplement, but given it is largely composed of polyunsaturated fats (PUFAs), do not cook with it as it is prone to rancidity and oxidation when exposed to heat. If you're a meat eater though, it is arguably better to opt for a good quality fish oil as evidence shows that the human body doesn't convert ALA to the active forms, EPA and DHA, as efficiently as we'd like.

High oleic sunflower oil

While the low-carb high-fat protocol avoids the seed oils due to their high levels of polyunsaturated fats, which means they tend to oxidise easily, high-oleic sunflower oil is at least 82% oleic acid, the same monounsaturated fat found in olive oil, lard, and your very own adipose tissue, while being extremely low in PUFAs. It has a slight nutty flavour, which makes it good to use in salad dressings as well as baked goods.

Macadamia nut oil

Comprising mostly monounsaturated fat (like olive oil), this is becoming more readily available in South Africa and has a fairly high smoke point and an equal ratio of omega-6 to -3. Structural qualities aside, it has the same buttery, smooth, rich flavour of the whole nut, and is delicious in cookies and salad dressings as it imparts a very distinctive flavour.

MCT oil

MCT (medium-chain triglyceride) oil is derived from coconut or palm oil and contains fatty acids with shorter carbon chains than most fats which are LCTs or long-chain fatty acids. 'Triglycerides' are in effect fatty acids, so an MCT is otherwise known as a MCFA (medium-chain fatty acid) in case you come across that term. While natural sources of MCTs, like coconut, contain the full range of MCTs (lauric acid, caproic acid, caprylic acid and capric acid), most MCT oils are made up of caprylic acid and capric acid only. MCT oil is not an oil found in nature, but is produced by separating out the medium-chain fatty acids from the rest of the oil, through an industrial process of 'fractionation'.

It remains liquid at all temperatures despite being a highly saturated fat due to the removal of the lauric acid as noted above, and is treated differently by the body than the LCTs. Instead of being metabolised through the digestion process like other fats are, MCTs are taken straight to the liver where they act in a very similar way to carbohydrates, providing instant but well-sustained energy. This makes MCTs more ketogenic. In enhancing ketone production, MCTs are

considered to improve blood sugar regulation, metabolism (especially fat metabolism), brain functioning and appetite regulation, and may also improve thyroid functioning.

MCT oil is neutral in taste and can be used to cook or bake with, and of course in your smoothies or to bullet-proof the coffee that kick-starts your day!

Olive oil

A corner stone of the Mediterranean diet, olive oil is a predominantly monounsaturated fat, which has been proven to raise HDL cholesterol and lower the amount of oxidised LDL cholesterol circulating in your bloodstream. Fruitiness and pepperiness can vary quite considerably depending on country of origin, type of olive pressed and the process used. South Africa is producing some really wonderful, internationally awarded oils, so experiment until you find one that feels right for you. The same rules apply – go for organic, cold-pressed versions.

When it comes to unsaturated fats like olive oil, avocado oil and similar others, it is important to keep them in an environment where they are less likely to oxidise and go rancid. The main drivers behind oxidative damage of cooking oils are heat, oxygen and light. Therefore, buy them in opaque glass containers and keep them in a cool, dry, dark place, making certain the lid is tightly screwed on again as soon as you're done using them.

Sesame oil

With a great distinctive flavour, but comprising 43% PUFAs, sesame oil is also one to be used occasionally, as part of a salad dressing blend, for quick stir-fries and in some baked goods.

Walnut oil

This is a most delicious nut oil, which is, however, high in omega-6s, so it's best kept as an occasional ingredient splashed over salads.

Flours

Almond flour or meal (see Building Blocks section for how to make your own) is one of the key ingredients in most low-carb baking. Almond flour/meal is higher in overall calories and fat and is lower in carbs than coconut flour, but doesn't have the same levels of fibre. Coconuts contain MUFA fatty acids and thus they are low in omega-6 fats, while nuts in general add omega-6 fats to your diet. Coconut flour absorbs more water than almond flour does due to its high-fibre content, is denser, and creates a softer product than almond flour. Almond flour also has a stronger taste and tastes like almonds, while coconut flour has a milder taste. I like to combine these two types of flours as they balance one another out in some respects!

Apart from the obvious use of these alternative flours in baked goods, you can use either to crumb fish or chicken, and in lieu of breadcrumbs in toppings and stuffings. Store your almond and coconut flour in an airtight container in the fridge or freezer to keep it fresh for longer after opening.

Arrowroot 'flour' or powder is a fine powdery substance that is made from the roots of a tropical plant widely cultivated in the Philippines, Caribbean islands and South America. It's a starch, but a very digestible one which contains very good levels of the B-complex group of vitamins such as niacin, thiamin, pyridoxine, pantothenic acid and riboflavin. Many of these vitamins take part as substrates for enzymes in carbohydrate, protein and fat metabolism in the body. We use it in small amounts to help 'stick' gluten-free baked goods together while adding some tenderness along the way.

Flax meal is also used extensively in low-carb baking as a form of 'flour' (see Building Blocks and below for more info on the nutritional qualities of flax). Be aware that it oxidises quite easily, so make up smallish quantities of flax meal at a time and store it in your fridge.

Fruits

Although the low-carb diet means that most fruits are off the table due to their fructose content and thus their GI, there are some that offer the highest ORAC values you can get in almost all foods and so their sugar content needs to be balanced against their overall nutritional value. While one would avoid the high-GI fruits, like mango, banana, grapes, figs and apricots, especially the dried versions such as raisins, sultanas and dates, it's the berry family in particular that offers not only nutritionally dense little packages, but loads of flavour in all manner of foods, from smoothies, to salads, sauces and desserts.

Apples are composed mostly of carbs but are also high in fibre, so while they have a GI of just under 40, the GL sits at around 6. They are also great sources of Vitamin C and various other antioxidants and potassium.

Lemons are a great source of Vitamin C and fibre, and contain many plant compounds, minerals and essential oils. Their citric acid content can increase the absorption of iron from other foods and also decreases the risk of kidney stones by diluting urine and increasing urine output.

As noted above, berries are really where it's at in the low-carb orchard, with most sitting at about the same GI levels as apples, but lower on the GL scale. Strawberries are over 90% water and low in carbs (net digestible carbohydrate content is less than 6 grams for every 100 grams), but very rich in Vitamin C (a powerful antioxidant) and other active plant compounds. They are also an excellent source of manganese, folate (B9) and potassium.

The ORAC score of blueberries is an incredible 9 621, which makes it one of the highest antioxidant foods we can eat. Not only are blueberries rich in antioxidants as a whole, but they are especially rich in proanthocyanidins, which are considered to play a role in reversing inflammation and to have valuable anti-aging properties.

Cranberries are members of the heather family and are related to blueberries, bilberries and lingonberries. With a high water content, they are composed mostly of carbs, but with high levels of insoluble fibre, which passes through the gastrointestinal tract pretty much intact. They're loaded with Vitamin C and antioxidants, in particular quercetin, and A-type proanthocyanidins, which have also been proven to be useful as a prevention against urinary tract infections. They're great used occasionally in baked goods such as muffins or desserts like crumbles, where you can mix them with apples or other berries.

Right from way back, goji berries have been considered little packets of nutritional dynamite in Tibetan and Chinese medicine. Unique among fruits, they contain all essential amino acids, and consequently have the highest concentration of protein of any fruit. They are also loaded with Vitamin C, contain more carotenoids than any other food, 21 trace minerals, and are high in fibre. Boasting 15 times the amount of iron found in spinach, as well as calcium, zinc, selenium and many other important trace minerals, this amazing superfruit also contains natural anti-inflammatory, anti-bacterial and anti-fungal compounds, and their powerful antioxidant properties and polysaccharides help to boost the immune system.

Be aware though that most of the stock available locally comes from the commercial-growing regions of China and Tibet, and contains high levels of pesticides and synthetic fertilisers, so soak them in warm water a few times to remove residue as much as possible before using. This softens them for use in smoothies and baking and you can always dry them out again afterwards if you're going to use them for trail mixes and granolas.

Herbs and spices

These add so much flavour to your cooking and can truly change a relatively arbitrary dish into something quite sublime. Herbs and spices not only add to the taste profile, they can also add to the nutritional value of a meal, even though we only use them in small amounts.

Hunt for non-irradiated spices if you can as most commercially packaged spices are exposed to radiation in order to destroy any microorganisms, bacteria, viruses or insects that might be present in them. While irradiation works to kill bacteria, it also disrupts the structure of everything it passes through. Specifically, irradiation breaks up a food's DNA, vitamins, minerals and proteins and creates 'free radicals' which we really want to minimise.

The array of herbs and spices available in our global village of today is quite spectacular really. Below is a little more info on some of my personal favourites.

Basil

This typically Mediterranean herb contains many polyphenolic flavonoids and essential oils, compounds which are known to have anti-inflammatory and anti-bacterial properties. 100 g of fresh leaves contains an astounding 5 275 mg or 175% of daily recommended doses of Vitamin A. Basil is also an excellent source of iron, containing 3.17 mg/100 g of fresh leaves. Choose fresh organic basil over the dried form of the herb as fresh leaves are so way ahead in quality and flavour and the typically radiation-treated dried basil shows significantly decreased Vitamin C and carotene levels. Add at the last moment when cooking, as prolonged cooking results in evaporation of its essential oils.

Black pepper

This is one I would really struggle to live without, given the way it impacts on any dish, enhancing and deepening the flavours with a little kick. Black pepper is the whole, partially ripened fruit of the *Piper nigrum* plant, while green pepper is the unripe fruit and white pepper is the completely ripe berry soaked in brine in order to remove its dark, outer skin. Native to southern India, black pepper sparked the start of the spice trade between Asia and Europe and was once used as a currency. Medicinally, it has been in use for centuries for its anti-inflammatory, carminative, anti-flatulent properties. Black pepper is a powerful antioxidant and is also antibacterial, and helps to break down and digest fats and meat proteins much more easily, by inducing the production of saliva and gastric juices needed for digestion in the stomach.

The strong flavour that characterises this spice is a function of the volatile oils, such as piperine that they contain, and these may evaporate if kept open in the air for extended periods. Thus, as with most spices, buy whole rather than ground as this way you'll also know there's nothing else in the mix and when you do grind them, they'll be fresh. Keep your whole peppercorns in a sealed container away from light and heat and they will last pretty much indefinitely.

Cardamom

This is one the most expensive spices by weight after saffron and vanilla. Rich in antioxidants, as are the other members of the ginger family, medicinally it has a host of values and helps relieve digestive problems induced by garlic and onion, which is one of the reasons we see it used so often in culinary traditions which incorporate those two ingredients. Distinctively aromatic, try to find whole green pods and then grind the seeds therein 'to order' by cracking open the pods and tipping the seeds into a spice or coffee grinder.

Chilli

Chilli peppers are rich in antioxidant plant compounds that have been linked with various health benefits. Most notable is capsaicin, which is what delivers the pungent and hot taste of chilli peppers. Capsaicin also has thermogenic properties that increase your blood flow and metabolism. Wash fresh chillies and remove seeds for a milder taste.

Cinnamon

Cinnamon goes way back into the mists of time with its use recorded in ancient Egypt around 4000 BC as a perfuming agent during their sacred embalming process.

The ORAC value of ground cinnamon is 131 420, which places it at 7 on the ranking of all antioxidant foods.

It contains a particular form of antioxidants called polyphenols that boost levels of three key proteins responsible for insulin signalling, glucose transport and inflammatory response, and as such it helps manage blood sugar levels by increasing insulin sensitivity. Apart from assisting with insulin resistance, cinnamon benefits the lipid profile and liver enzymes and its essential oils also qualify it as an 'anti-microbial' food, given its ability to help stop the growth of bacteria as well as fungi (including the commonly problematic yeast *Candida*). Cinnamon has been shown to be especially beneficial in treating digestive disorders, menstrual discomfort and joint pain because of its high content of cinnamaldehyde (the anti-inflammatory molecular compound that gives cinnamon its flavour and aroma).

Cinnamon should be kept in a tightly sealed glass container in a cool, dark and dry place. Ground cinnamon will keep for about six months, while cinnamon sticks will stay fresh for about one year stored this way.

Clove

Clove's unique phytonutrient components are accompanied by an incredible variety of valuable nutrients – it is an excellent source of manganese, a very good source of Vitamin K and dietary fibre, and a good source of iron, magnesium and calcium. Intense in smell and taste, this one is to be used with caution. Remember that you can always add, but once you've thrown it in, there's no reducing its imprint! Buy whole and grind on demand if you can, although ground cloves will keep for about six months. Cloves should be kept in a tightly sealed glass container in a cool, dark and dry place.

Coriander

When it's fresh I guess it's technically a herb, but when we're talking about the seeds, either whole or ground, it becomes a spice! Fresh coriander clocks in at 5 100 with its ORAC score, just below that of blackberries and is rich in phytonutrients, flavonoids and phenolic compounds, including vitamins A, K, potassium and folate. Interestingly from a blood-sugar control perspective, a study published in the *Journal of Food Sciences* showed that when diabetes has been diagnosed, coriander helps support healthy liver function, and helps to balance blood sugar. Health-giving benefits aside, it also adds amazing flavour, irrespective of the form you use it in.

Garlic

This has been recognised in many cultures for its medicinal properties as well as its culinary value. Garlic is rich in phytonutrients, minerals, vitamins and antioxidants, in particular the flavonoid types such as carotene beta, zea-xanthin, and vitamins like B6 and C. Garlic has been shown to lower blood triglycerides and cholesterol and can also reduce platelet aggregation, which theoretically could lower the risk of stroke. It is full of an active sulphur compound known as allicin, which whacks microbes like bacteria and fungi, and helps to boost the immune system.

To reduce the potent aftertaste and sour breath that can accompany a garlicky meal, try slicing the garlic cloves vertically and removing the green bit at the centre. Rinsing the chopped garlic under water will also help to remove some of the sulphur. Eating some parsley, yoghurt or milk and even cracking a few cardamom seeds or a bit of anise or fennel seed in your mouth also helps after the fact. Chewing or sucking on a slice of lemon or orange also helps as the citric acid will keep the mouth moist with saliva, preventing the growth of bacteria that causes bad breath. Then green and peppermint teas contain polyphenols that reduce the volatile sulphur compounds that the garlic produces.

Dry bulbs can be stored at room temperature in a cool dark environment away from humidity where they stay in good condition for several weeks.

Ginger

Part of the plant family that includes turmeric and cardamom, ginger has been used for thousands of years as an effective digestive aid and natural remedy for nausea. It not only promotes regular digestion and metabolism of your food but also assists in promoting a strong immune system. The anti-inflammatory benefits of ginger come largely from gingerols, the oily resin from the root that acts as a highly potent antioxidant and anti-inflammatory agent and which are known to enhance insulin sensitivity. The total antioxidant strength of ginger root measured in terms of the ORAC system is 14 840 µmol TE/100 g. It contains many essential nutrients and vitamins such as pyridoxine (Vitamin B6), pantothenic acid (Vitamin B5) and goodly amounts of minerals like potassium, manganese, copper and magnesium, potassium being an important component of cell and body fluids that helps control heart rate and blood pressure.

Use fresh ginger rather than the dried powdered form as gingerol levels are higher, and look for tender, pale and even-skinned roots that feel heavy in your hand as these are fresher. Put the fresh root through your juicer to add an amazing zing to your veggie juices, grate it into casseroles and add it to curries. It pairs beautifully with dark chocolate too. Fresh ginger can be stored in the fridge for up to three weeks if it is left unpeeled.

Galangal, also known as blue ginger, is a closely related herb that is used extensively in East Asian regions, especially in Thai, Malaysian and Indonesian cuisine. Galangal has a mild, subtle flavour and is less pungent than ginger, but this is not as easy to find fresh as is ginger.

Mustard
Since mustard seed is a stimulant, it initiates a warming of the circulatory system. This can result in dilated blood vessels, and a warmed system can help burn and metabolise fat in the body. As a warming herb, mustard seed will encourage perspiration that can lower fevers and cleanse the body of toxins. If you're using a prepared mustard paste as opposed to the seeds or ground seed, read the label to make sure you're happy with all the other ingredients in the mix.

Salt
Most 'table' salt has been chemically processed by taking natural salt and heating it to 1 200°F/650°C. During this extreme process, the chemical composition is completely altered and all of the nutritional benefits are destroyed, leaving in inorganic sodium chloride to which is then added anti-caking agents and other unnatural stuff. Even sea salt is now problematic, given the levels of toxins such as mercury in the oceans. 'Real' raw and natural salt contains 60 trace minerals which help with hydration, sufficient sodium levels to help balance your sodium-potassium ratios, electrolytes

like magnesium and other trace elements that help with adrenal, immune and thyroid function. I like to work with Himalayan salt specifically, but we have a great local source of natural salt in the Kalahari, so look out for these options. Flavour-wise, they're light years away from the mass-produced stuff.

Sumac
Native to the Middle East, sumac is derived from a plant that produces deep red berries, which are then dried and ground into coarse powder. It has a tangy, lemony flavour and adds zing and wonderful colour to roasts, marinades and dressing. Sprinkle it over a dish just before serving for maximum visual and taste impact.

Turmeric
Turmeric, known officially as *Curcuma longa* and historically as Indian saffron, is a rhizome of the ginger family. Apart from adding colour and flavour, the active ingredient in turmeric, curcumin, switches on the liver genes that keep glucose levels in check by improving the pancreas's ability to make insulin and helping to slow down the metabolism of carbohydrates after meals. It also inhibits the genetic switches that allow for cancerous cell growth to occur and enhances cellular energy to speed metabolism.

While not easy to find, fresh turmeric is occasionally available and is delightful to work with. Beware that the powdered form has a tendency to land everywhere, so make sure you're wrapped up in an apron that covers your front and pull up your sleeves when working with it!

Vanilla
Vanilla beans are the dried seed pods of the vanilla vine, containing an oily and unctuous gloop of miniscule little seeds. The darker the bean, the higher the quality. If you don't have a vanilla bean to slice open, then keep a good vanilla extract on hand, which, while it's more expensive than

the commercial and artificial 'essence', has a very particular quality and a depth of flavour that is very special.

Za'atar

Za'atar is used to denote both a family of herbs and a herb, *Thymbra spicata*, with a slight minty tendency, in the marjoram/oregano family. It is also the name of a dried herb blend, which combines a particular wild type of thyme, along with marjoram and oregano, sesame seeds, salt, a little cumin perhaps and sumac. It is used throughout North Africa and the Middle East to add flavour to breads, meats and veggies.

Nuts

Nuts by definition are the seeds of fruits, encased in a hard outer shell. They grow on flowering upright trees and shrubs, which is why a peanut, growing on the ground, is not actually a nut! Although they're high in calories, nuts are incredibly energy-dense, so a little goes a long way. One of the biggest benefits nuts have to offer is their gamma-tocopherol content. Gamma-tocopherol is a type of Vitamin E that acts as a powerful antioxidant, fighting free radical damage and oxidative stress that are linked to many chronic illnesses and to cancer in particular.

To get maximum nutrition it is best to soak them before they are eaten and then roast them, which can reduce phytate levels (see Building Blocks section). Roasting also releases the oils, making them immensely more flavourful in my opinion, while killing off any bacterial residue on the skin. Always toast nuts in a shallow container in a single layer in a low to moderate oven – the nuts are 'done' when you can smell their aroma and they've become golden brown. Transfer them to a cool surface immediately, to minimise any carryover cooking. Given their high oil content, they can both scorch and turn rancid quickly, so stay focused

while toasting and then keep them in a well-sealed jar in a cool, dark place. Raw nuts can even be stored in the freezer if you buy in bulk.

Almonds

Originally native to the Middle East and South Asia, almonds are actually stone fruits related to cherries, plums and peaches. California now produces 80% of the world's almonds, which means they have most likely been pasteurised or irradiated. That said they're possibly the most nutrient-dense nuts. Almonds are also the only nuts that are alkaline and, gram for gram, they contain the highest level of calcium of all nuts. They're rich in protein and dietary fibre, antioxidants and vitamins such as riboflavin and Vitamin E, and minerals such as magnesium, copper and selenium, as well as potassium, calcium, phosphorous and iron.

They contain over 20 flavonoids that enhance the effects of Vitamin E and 70% of their fat is monounsaturated which means their consumption helps slow the rate at which glucose (sugar) is released into the bloodstream. However, like all nuts they contain phytates which can make them difficult to digest. Almonds are one of only a few nuts that will actually sprout when soaked (soaking them neutralises the phytate, allowing the nutrients from the nut to be released – see Building Blocks section).

Brazils

Brazil nuts contain protein, fibre, Vitamin E, copper, niacin, magnesium and selenium. It is their incredible selenium levels that are the most obvious benefit of Brazil nuts, as unless you're regularly eating animal kidneys and wild salmon, selenium is not the easiest mineral to come by.

Cashews

The cashew 'nut' is actually a seed that is harvested from the cashew fruit. Native to Brazil's Amazon rain forest, cashews were spread all over the planet by Portuguese explorers. They're high in calories, though also high in soluble dietary fibre, vitamins, minerals and monounsaturated fatty acids like oleic and palmitoleic acids. They have a higher ratio of carb to fat content though, so use them sparingly.

Hazelnuts

Hazelnuts are rich in vitamins E and B, arginine and manganese, as well as being one of the richest sources of polyphenolic acid (a type of anti-oxidant) and the plant sterol beta-sitosterol, which helps to lower cholesterol. Hazelnuts also contain an especially high amount of proanthocyanidins, which are compounds found in plants that are believed to have anti-inflammatory and other health benefits such as helping to reduce cardiovascular disease, lower blood pressure and prevent dementia. But wait, there's more – they're also high in monounsaturated fatty acids like *oleic* as well as the essential fatty acid, *linoleic acid* that helps lower LDL and increase HDL cholesterol, and they are exceptionally rich in folate, which is a unique feature for nuts. And they have to be just one of the most delicious things on the planet!

Buy them in their skins, roast gently, cool and rub off the skin. Store the shelled nuts (without their outer coat) inside an airtight container and place in the fridge to avoid them turning rancid.

Macadamia nuts

These are high in antioxidants, protein, fibre, MUFAs (86% of the fat in this delicious nut is monounsaturated), magnesium and potassium. They are low in phytate, so there is no need to soak or sprout and they're also generally low in pesticide residue courtesy of their incredibly thick shell. They are a very good source of phytosterols such as ß-sitosterol but they're not so low in calories though, so be careful about throwing too many down your gullet – 100 g of nuts provides

about 718 calories, which is one of the highest values among nuts.

Pecans

Pecan nuts, like the fruit of all other members of the *hickory* genus, are not true nuts but botanically fruits (drupe). Rich in monounsaturated fatty acids like oleic acid and an excellent source of phenolic antioxidants, adding pecan nuts to the diet is considered to help to decrease *total* as well as *LDL* while increasing *HDL* cholesterol levels in the blood. A 30 g-odd serving of pecans provides 3 grams of dietary fibre and over 19 vitamins and minerals including vitamins A and E, calcium, potassium, thiamin, magnesium, iron and zinc. Their delicious buttery flavour is enhanced with roasting and they pair beautifully with something that is a little tart, such as goji or cranberries in granolas or muffins for example, as well as a topping for salads.

Pine nuts

Pine nuts are an excellent source of vitamins E and K, copper, and iron, all of which support heart health. Furthermore, pine nuts are an excellent source of monounsaturated fat. They cost so much 'cos they're such a pain to grow and harvest. They are, however, sublime and so well worth it. Again, they're infinitely tastier if dry roasted, and need to be protected from heat to prevent them going rancid.

Pistachios

After plantation it takes approximately eight to ten years until the pistachio tree produces its first major crop, which might explain in part why they're one of the most expensive nuts on the planet. They are, however, also one of the nuts that are relatively low in phytic acid, and they're a great source of prebiotic fibre and so help reduce post-prandial glucose. They're a rich source of energy – 100 g of kernels carries 557 calories – but they offer good amounts of monounsaturated fatty acids like oleic acid and antioxidants, copper and manganese. They're also an excellent source of Vitamin E and are especially rich in gamma-tocopherol. Vitamin E is a powerful lipid-soluble antioxidant essential for maintaining the integrity of cell membranes of mucosa and skin and it's a great scavenger of harmful-free oxygen radicals.

Try to buy unshelled (with intact outer coat) whole nuts instead of processed ones that are free from cracks and uniform in colour. Raw, unshelled pistachios can be stored in a cool dry place for many months. However, shelled kernels should be placed in an airtight container and kept inside the fridge in order to prevent them turning rancid.

Walnuts

Widely used in baking and in many of the wonderful savoury dishes of the Middle East, Turkey and the Caucasus, walnuts are delicate creatures whose shape mirrors that of our brains. Walnuts are being touted as a new superfood, loaded as they are with omega-3 fatty acids. They contain the highest amount of alpha-linolenic acid (ALA), the plant-based omega-3 essential fatty acid, known for its anti-inflammatory properties and role in heart health. They also contain high levels of vitamins B6 and E, ellagic acid and L-arginine, an essential amino acid that the body uses to produce nitric oxide, necessary for keeping blood vessels flexible. Linoleic acid helps reduce body fat and weight, lowers cholesterol and boosts the immune system and brain function. Ellagic acid is a powerful antioxidant that combats cancer, and L-arginine promotes healing and detoxification. 100 g of these nuts carries a score of 13 541 µmol TE (Trolex equivalents) on the ORAC scale which makes them super heroes in the fight against free radicals.

As with most nuts, unshelled walnuts can be stored in a cool dry place for many months, whereas shelled kernels should be placed inside airtight containers and kept inside the fridge to avoid them turning rancid.

Psyllium husk

Historically used to assist with constipation, psyllium finds its place in the low-carb pantry based on the fact that it can be difficult to get enough fibre in a diet when you eliminate the carbohydrates in cereals, whole grains and fruits. It is essentially a form of dietary fibre, with every 100 grams of psyllium delivering 71 grams of soluble fibre that helps provide bulk and in fact also helps gluten-free goods stick together. Studies reported in *The American Journal of Clinical Nutrition* have shown psyllium to be quite effective in lowering total as well as LDL cholesterol levels, which can be helpful to those with high cholesterol and those at increased risk for developing hypercholesterolaemia, such as people with Type-2 diabetes.

Raising agents

Baking powder

Like yeast and baking soda (below), baking powder is a leavening agent, which is a combination of baking soda and either citric or tartaric acid or both. As with baking soda, once it has been combined with other wet ingredients it must be baked immediately. Baking powder can lose its strength over time so it should be tested if it has been sitting on the shelf for a while. Good baking powder will bubble strongly when one teaspoon of it is mixed with one-quarter cup of hot water.

Baking soda

Also known as bicarbonate of soda, baking soda reacts with an acid when it is wet to produce carbon dioxide and lighten baked goods. The wet, acidic ingredients that typically cause this reaction with baking soda in a batter include buttermilk, sour milk, citrus juices, chocolate, vinegar or honey, and the reaction will begin immediately when liquids are added to the dry ingredients – so goods incorporating baking soda should be baked as soon as they've been stirred together (unlike yeast where the carbon dioxide release is lower which is why goods made with yeast are left to 'prove').

Yeast

Dry yeast is the form most readily available and is stable until it meets moisture and warmth. It feeds on starches and sugars, which is why we don't really use it in low-carb baking. With candida so prevalent, and many of us not having the healthiest of gut flora, it's best to avoid this if we can.

Seeds

Seeds are an integral part of the low-carb diet, but easy to over-consume, and being pretty much universally high in phytic acid and omega-6s you do need to exercise a little caution.

Chia

Known as the running food by the Aztecs, these little seeds were used for centuries as a staple food by the Indians. Chia has the ability to absorb more than 12 times its weight in water and helps to regulate the body's absorption of nutrients and body fluids in part through their high content of electrolytes. With good levels of protein, chia is also high in omega-3 fatty acids – ALA in particular – so they're great for both muscle repair and blood sugar control. Chia is also useful for thickening smoothies given their absorptive powers.

Flax or linseed

Flax seeds are one of the richest sources of the plant-based omega-3 fatty acids, known as alpha-linolenic acid (ALA), which we now know is an important element in fighting cancer and cardiovascular disease. The ALA in flax can help protect the lining of the digestive tract and maintain gastro-intestinal health. High in both soluble and unsoluble fibre, they also help to trap fat and cholesterol in the digestive system so that it is unable to be absorbed. Flax seeds contain really high levels of lignans, which are unique fibre-related polyphenols that provide us with antioxidant benefits for anti-aging, hormone balance and cellular health. Polyphenols support the growth of probiotics in the gut and thus may also help manage candida in the body.

Phytic acid levels are high though and the whole flax is somewhat difficult to digest, so to make the flax components more bioavailable, it's better to mill it before using. Flax seeds also have a higher ratio of omega-6 than -3 (a good rate is 1:1) and contain phytoestrogens, which in some people can affect the hormonal balance.

Hemp seed

These little power houses contain a 3:1 ratio of omega-3 and omega-6 fatty acids. In fact they are one of the few sources of stearidonic acid, an intermediate omega-3 fat in the conversion pathway from ALA to EPA with the ability to increase the EPA content of red blood cells in humans.

They're also loaded with magnesium and copper, and are high in tocopherols, and unique antioxidants. They have a nice nutty taste and in fact constitute a 'perfect protein' as they not only contain all 20 amino acids, but also each of the 9 *essential* amino acids that our bodies cannot produce. In fact, just 2 tablespoons of hemp seed will deliver 10 g of protein, so think about adding them to smoothies.

They are rich in soluble and unsoluble fibre which naturally cleanses the colon and reduces sugar cravings and their GLA content helps with hormonal regulation. Be not afraid – while derived from the same plant as cannabis, hemp seeds do NOT cause any psychotropic reaction!

Poppy seed

Obtained from the dry fruits (pods) of the poppy plant (yes, we're talking about the opium poppy), these seeds are especially rich in oleic and linoleic acids, show good levels of minerals, are an excellent source of B-complex vitamins, and a good source of dietary fibre. They are high in polyunsaturated fats, however, which make them vulnerable to oxidation and so need to be stored in a cool, dark place. Gently roasting them in a pan under mild heat releases the special aromatic essential oils in the seeds and adds to their flavour and crunchiness.

Pumpkin seed or pepitas

Toasted pumpkin seeds are a sublime snack and although high in phytic acid and PUFAs, they have a nice mineral profile, lots of fibre as well as being a source of important essential amino acids such as tryptophan and glutamate. Tryptophan is converted into serotonin and niacin, and serotonin is a beneficial neuro-chemical often labelled as nature's sleeping pill. Their high caloric value mainly comes from protein and fats, in particular monounsaturated fatty acids (MUFAs) like oleic acid (18:1) that helps lower LDL cholesterol and increases HDL cholesterol in the blood. Hulled pumpkin kernels deteriorate soon if exposed to warm, humid conditions, so store in an airtight container inside the fridge or before toasting in the freezer.

Sesame seed

One of the first oil seeds known to humankind, sesame seeds are especially rich in the monounsaturated fatty acid, oleic acid. They are also a very valuable source of dietary protein with fine quality amino acids that are essential for growth, especially in children – just 100 g of seeds provides about 18 g of protein. Sesame is rich in quality vitamins and minerals, especially B-complex vitamins such as niacin and folic acid, with many essential minerals including calcium, phosphorus, iron, manganese, zinc, magnesium, selenium and copper.

Tahini is the butter or paste made from grinding up sesame seeds, just as you'd make a nut butter. This is delicious added to salad dressings (dilute raw tahini with water and place in the blender along with a little olive oil, some lemon juice, black pepper and Himalayan salt) or drizzled over grilled zucchini or aubergine. Given the fact that they are high in unsaturated fats, they should be stored in airtight containers in a cool place to avoid them turning rancid.

Sunflower seed

With 50% of their fatty acids being PUFAs, they nevertheless contain decent levels of MUFAs as well, along with some fine-quality amino acids, with a mere 100 g of seeds providing about 21 g of protein. They're also relatively high in phytosterols which lower cholesterol, and in polyphenol and Vitamin E, both of which are powerful anti-oxidants. With loads of niacin, folic acid and essential minerals, they're also full of dietary fibre, and are especially delicious roasted with some herbs and spices and tossed over salads or added to bread mixes.

Sweeteners

Erythritol

This is one of the sugar alcohols, like maltitol, mannitol, sorbitol and xylitol (see below), which is about 60–80% as sweet as sucrose (table sugar). The sugar alcohols are not to be confused with artificial sweeteners, occurring naturally in plants, like fruits and vegetables. They provide a sweet taste without raising blood sugar to the degree that sucrose does as they convert to glucose more slowly in your body and do not require much insulin to metabolise. What makes erythritol my preferred sugar replacement is that it is noncaloric, is derived from a fermentation process and is heat stable and doesn't cause the tummy upset that xylitol can.

Honey

Honey consists of dextrose and fructose (broken down from sucrose through the honey bee's digestion) in a nearly 1:1 ratio, with other components such as water, wax, nutrients, etc. Honey is considered by many to be a 'functional food' though, which means it is a natural food with health benefits. It contains natural antioxidants, enzymes and minerals including iron, zinc, potassium, calcium, phosphorous, magnesium and selenium. Vitamins found in honey include Vitamin B6, thiamin, riboflavin, pantothenic acid and niacin. In addition, the nutraceuticals contained in honey help neutralise damaging-free radical activity.

Thus incorporating small amounts of raw, unprocessed honey, given its nutritional profile, has its place. While different honeys have different glycemic indexes, a safe average value is 50, so use it sparingly. Avoid commercial honey as it is often heavily processed and may even have been chemically refined. These filtering and refining processes usually involve heat which destroys the natural enzymes, vitamins and minerals in honey and eliminates many of the beneficial phytonutrients including pollen and enzyme-rich propolis. Unlike raw, processed honey clocks in much higher on the GI score at around 75 and is definitely to be avoided.

Stevia

Stevia is a zero-calorie sweetener derived from a green, leafy plant that is native to South America. You can buy whole or ground stevia leaves, but most often you are getting an extract (either liquid or powder), which is a refined version of the plant's isolated sweet compounds, which is hundreds of times sweeter than sugar – 1 teaspoon of stevia extract can have a similar sweetening power as a whole cup of sugar so go gently. It has an aftertaste though, which I find too intrusive, but play with it to see how your tongue responds.

Xylitol

Sugar alcohols are like hybrids of a sugar molecule and an alcohol molecule, with a structure that gives them the ability to stimulate the sweet taste receptors on the tongue. With 40% fewer calories than table sugar or sucrose (table sugar has 4 calories per gram vs 2.4 calories per gram for xylitol), it doesn't contain any vitamins, minerals or protein so in that sense its calories are 'empty'. That said, sugar substitutes are really useful when we need a little sweetness in our lives. Look out for xylitol that has been processed from trees like birch (often called birch xylitol), rather than the kind produced from xylan in an industrial process. It can have an effect on the digestive tract, though this usually settles over time and if you use it sparingly. It is *highly toxic* to dogs though, with 0.3 g enough to make a Chihuahua sick. So don't *ever* hand Fido some of the treats you've baked with it, *please*.

Xylitol is available in a crystalline and a syrup form, which is useful as these different forms are better in different dishes, so it's nice to have both in your pantry.

Vegetables

With fruit largely out of the equation, vegetables take on an even more significant role in a low-carb diet, bringing balance to the protein and fat ratios. And while it's perfectly simple to check up on the GI and GL levels of different veggies, remember too that it is the overall nutritional profile that is important.

Kale, for example, is arguably among one of the most nutritious vegetables you can eat, calorie for calorie, with a 100 g serving delivering only 50 calories and 10 g carbs (2 of which are fibre).

Without the oxalates you find in spinach, kale contains 10 times the RDA of Vitamin K1, twice the RDA for Vitamin C and 3 times the RDA for Vitamin A (from beta-carotene), and more calcium gram for gram than milk. Work with it like you would spinach, which means you can pan it, use it raw in salads, and juice it. And if you haven't eaten kale chips yet, you haven't lived.

Explore other interesting greens like collard, chicory, Swiss chard, Chinese cabbage and watercress to bring some diversity into the greens mix.

Pumpkin and butternut are another area of interest as they present a classic case where you really need to understand how the glycemic load takes into account both the GI value and the amount of carbohydrates that a food contains. Butternut squash has a GI ranking of 51 and a GL of 3. Pumpkin, while having a higher GI at 75, also has a GL of 3, which means that in both cases you would have to consume a large amount of either to increase your blood sugar significantly. Both are rich in dietary fibre, antioxidants, minerals, vitamins – especially Vitamin A which is required by the body for maintaining the integrity of skin and mucusa – and is also an essential vitamin for good visual sight.

Sweet potatoes are another 'carby' kind of veg which are fortunately also high in fibre (a 100 g serving delivers about 3 g), which slows the absorption of sugar and helps to deliver a feeling of satiety. They are also rich in beta-carotene, which is transformed into Vitamin A in the body, in vitamins C and E, as well as in potassium and manganese and certain of the B-group vitamins. The antioxidant activity of sweet potatoes increases as the flesh increases in orange colour, so look out for 'orange' sweet potato or kumara, and use this form over the usual white sweet potato.

Sea vegetables are another great category to look at, loaded with minerals such as magnesium, calcium, iron, zinc, potassium and manganese, and then of course the iodine that is very often lacking in modern diets. A great way to make sure you don't lack iodine is to eat some form of seaweed once or twice a week. While some of the other forms such as kombu and wakame are higher in nutritional punch, nori is more readily available. Cut it into strips perhaps and toss over a salmon salad or incorporate it into an omelette. It's actually very tasty. Kelp is also available in flakes which are great sprinkled over foods and in powdered form, which you can add into green juices or soups, for example.

One last note on this topic is around the nightshade vegetables. Nightshades are a class of plants that contain a higher level of alkaloids (a naturally occurring toxin that protects the plant from predators) that can be harmful to nerve, muscle, gut and joint function. The more commonly consumed vegetables in this class are tomatoes, potatoes, okra, peppers and eggplant.

Nightshades contain types of alkaloids that can irritate the gastrointestinal system and act as acetylcholinesterase inhibitors thus affecting neurotransmitters. While many allergens are easy to single out – such as with nuts or dairy – those with sensitivities to nightshade vegetables often have similar complaints to those with gluten-sensitive reactions. Irritable bowel disorders and other gastrointestinal issues, heartburn, nerve sensitisation and joint pain are commonly associated with nightshade sensitivity. The capsaicin in chilli peppers is part of this group of alkaloids, and the heartburn and acid reflux some people experience on eating chillies arises as the capsaicin irritates the lining of the oesophagus and stomach. So if you know you're battling with leaky-gut syndrome or find yourself struggling with any of these symptoms, eliminate the nightshade family and see how your body responds.

If you're fortunate enough to have something of a garden, have a bash at planting some of your own veg, herbs and maybe even some strawberries. Tomatoes and pumpkins are fairly easy to get going, although you'll probably have to protect leafy greens from being enjoyed by some of the other creatures inhabiting your property.

Water

While some bottled water does indeed come from pristine sources, much of it is nothing more than municipal water, purified in some or other way and then branded, packaged and sold at a premium.

Irrespective of its purity or mineral profile, though, most bottled water comes in polyethylene terephthalate or PET bottles. Increasingly, research is showing that when stored in hot or warm temperatures, this form of plastic may leach its chemicals into the water. Of particular concern are phthalates, which are used to make plastic softer, and which function as endocrine disrupters, which means they block or mimic hormones, affecting the body's normal functions.

Apart from the impact on our own health, bottled water is shipped around the planet, expending valuable resources against what is questionably worth it in terms of being a 'purer' or 'healthier' product. While we are encouraged to cut down on our consumption of fossil fuels, bottled water increases them as virgin petroleum is used to make PET, and the more bottles we use, the more virgin petroleum will be needed to create new bottles. And that's not taking into account the fossil fuels that are burned to fill the bottles and distribute them. In fact the energy used each year making the bottles needed to meet the demand for bottled water in the United States alone is estimated as being equivalent to more than 17 million barrels of oil. That's enough to fuel over 1 million cars for a year!

Which is just an astonishing irony – as we allow our rivers and lakes to become ever more polluted by fuel and chemical runoff, we pay to drink water that is supposedly free of these pollutants. Yet these pollutants are increasingly entering our water supply because of the very bottles we're buying the 'purer' water in!

So if you're concerned about the quality of your tap water, there are many ways to filter out at least some of the impurities, whether you use a jug with a filter, a filter integrated into the tap, a counter-top filter, an under-sink filter or a whole-house water filter which filters water before it enters the household pipes. Different technologies exist, so explore the options that include carbon-activated, ceramic, ion exchange, mechanical filters, ozone, reverse osmosis and UV light systems. Any which way, rather than using plastic containers, carry your tap or filtered water in a stainless steel canteen or flask or a glass bottle.

A BAKER'S GLOSSARY

It may seem that many of the terms used in baking and in cooking in general have overtones of violence and abuse, which might be part of the reason they can also be a little confusing. Herewith a short list of some of the terms often used that will hopefully clarify things unambiguously!

Baking blind

This is the process of partially or fully baking a pastry case in the oven without the filling. Line a tart tin with pastry, cover it with greaseproof paper and weigh it down with ceramic baking beans or dried chickpeas, beans or lentils. Baking blind is ideal if you have a no-cook filling, a filling that needs little cooking or is cooked at a low temperature. It ensures a crisp finish.

Baking stone

This is a centimetre-odd-thick piece of porous stone or unglazed tile-like material that, when hot, draws moisture away from the bread or pizza dough placed on it, much like a brick-oven floor. When baked on a baking stone, hearth breads and pizza crusts emerge with a crisp, crunchy crust. The stone is placed on the lowest oven rack. Follow the manufacturer's directions as to whether preheating the stone with the oven is recommended.

Batter

Confused about what distinguishes a batter, from a mixture, from a dough? A batter is a mixture of flour, liquid and other ingredients *that is thin enough to pour.*

Beating

This is not a punishment but the rigorous mixing of ingredients using a wooden spoon, electric whisk, food mixer or food processor. The purpose is to thoroughly combine ingredients and to incorporate air, making cakes light and fluffy.

Beating egg whites properly is the key to creating certain extra-light cookies, and other treats such as macaroons. Three things to remember: the bowl and beaters must be clean and grease-free; use a stainless-steel, ceramic or glass bowl, not plastic; and egg whites will whip higher if they're at room temperature before beating.

When beating egg whites, at first you'll have a puddle of clear liquid with some large bubbles in it. Continue beating, and soon the whisk will begin to leave tracks in the bowl. Eventually, the whites will form 'stiff peaks'. To test the character of your whites, pull your whisk or beaters straight up out of the foam. It's extremely easy to go too far. When you start to see grainy white clumps, you're beyond stiff peaks, and every stroke of the whisk or beater is tearing apart the network of air, water and protein you've worked so hard to create. You'll also see a pool of clear liquid under the foam. The good news is that the foam on top of the liquid will essentially still work. The bad news is that you can't really fix what's happened, other than to start over with new egg whites.

Biga

An overnight starter that uses both domestic yeast and whatever wild yeast it can capture from the air as it sits. Biga is the Italian name for starter, and it can be either wet, with a consistency like pancake batter, or dry, like a stiff dough.

Creaming
This is the term used in baking for beating sugar and softened butter together to form a lighter-coloured mixture that is aerated. This is one of the ways to add lightness and volume to cakes.

Sugar and fat are beaten together to form and capture air bubbles, when the sugar crystals cut into fat molecules to make an air pocket. When you first start beating sugar and fat together, the mixture is thick and somewhat lumpy. As you continue to beat, the mixture becomes creamier in texture, more uniform, and lighter in colour as air is beaten in.

Curdling
Curdling is when a food mixture separates into its component parts. A creamed cake mixture may curdle if the eggs are added too quickly or are too cold.

Cutting in
This is not what incenses you on the way to work on the morning. To 'cut in' refers to the technique where two knives or a pastry blender is used to combine cold fats (butter or solid coconut oil, for example) with flour or sugar *without* creaming or mixing air in the ingredients. A crumbly- or grainy-looking mixture is what results.

Dough
Dough is a mixture of flour and liquids (and may have other ingredients) which is thick enough to be handled, kneaded or shaped.

Dusting/dredging
This involves sprinkling sugar or spices over food as a decoration or for additional flavour. A recipe may also ask you to 'dust' a work surface with flour to stop dough from sticking before kneading and rolling it out. A tea strainer or fine sieve is suitable for dusting. You can also buy a shaker or dredger, which consists of a cup with a handle and perforated lid.

Egg wash
This is a thoroughly combined mixture of 1 whole egg, egg yolk or egg white mixed with 1 tablespoon of cold water or milk. This mixture is brushed onto the unbaked surface of breads, pastries or other baked goods just before baking to provide a deeper colour or gloss to the crust.

Emulsify
Emulsifying means mixing two ingredients that might not normally go together willingly, such as oil and water. This is done by slowly adding one ingredient to the other while vigorously mixing or whisking. An emulsifier, on the other hand, is an ingredient such as an egg that, when beaten with two non-mixing ingredients like oil and vinegar, will hold them in a suspension so they do not separate.

Folding in
This is a technique used to gently combine a light, airy ingredient (such as beaten egg whites) with a heavier one (such as cake batter) in order to preserve as much of the added air as possible. The lighter mixture is poured on top of the heavier one in a large bowl. Starting at the back of the bowl, a metal spoon is used to cut down vertically through the two mixtures, across the bottom of the bowl and up the side. The bowl should be rotated slightly with each series of strokes. This down-across-up-and-over motion gently combines the ingredients to create a light, fluffy consistency.

Ghee
Ghee is the Indian term for clarified butter, which is butter that has had all the water and milk solids removed. It is 100% fat and can be stored for

considerably longer than butter. Store-bought ghee can be stored at room temperature for many months; clarified butter that you make yourself can be stored in the fridge for several months.

Lukewarm
How warm is lukewarm? It is officially around 105°F/40°C.

Making a well
Forming a 'well' in dry ingredients and adding the wet ingredients is a way to combine dry and wet without over-mixing and without creating lumps, which is particularly useful when making pancake, muffin or cake batters. Move the dry ingredients to the sides of the bowl, leaving a depression in the centre in which the wet ingredients can pool. You can do this with a spoon, a spatula or your fingers. Once you've added the wet ingredients, you mix them into the dry ingredients gradually, by stirring around the edges of the pool until the ingredients are thoroughly combined.

Reduce
As the term suggests, this is about diminishing, but in cooking terms it's when a liquid is boiled steadily to reduce and thicken it by evaporating some of the water.

Resting the batter
After a vigorous round of beating, it's usually one's arm that needs resting, never mind the batter. Technically though, the consistency of whole-grain batters often benefits from extra time between mixing and baking. During this rest, the bran from the whole grain slowly absorbs some of the moisture in the batter. The result is a muffin or pancake with a smoother, less gritty texture; one that holds itself together better after being cooked. While this is less relevant to grain-free baking, there are elements like psyllium that benefit from a pause in the process. To 'rest

the batter', simply cover and refrigerate for the recommended amount of time before proceeding with the recipe. Dough in particular benefits from a brief (10–30 minutes) intermission in handling as it will be more easily rolled or shaped thereafter.

Scald
How hot is scalding? It's heating to near boiling stage. Scalding milk retards souring and incapacitates some of the enzymes that might otherwise retard yeast growth.

Simmer
It may well be the feeling you have when you've burnt rather than scalded the milk. That said, simmering a cooked liquid, broth or soup is bringing it to just below the boiling point. You'll know when it reaches that stage because small bubbles appear on the surface.

Softened
A solid, high-fat-content substance that has been brought to room temperature in order to make it more pliable. Softened butter is not melted butter, however, so do distinguish between the two.

Whip
Stir briskly with a whisk to incorporate air. See below!

Whisk
Noun: a kitchen tool made of wire loops that is used to add air as it mixes substances together. Verb: pretty much the same as whipping, above.

Zest
Zest is the thin, outer skin of a citrus fruit. It is fragrant and removed with a paring knife, vegetable peeler or citrus peeler so that it can be added to baked goods to add its delicious flavour. Keep your zest light and delicate though – bigger is not better in this particular instance.

CONVERSION CHARTS

We all draw on many sources when we're cooking and baking, and some recipes use measurement forms that are not common here.

And what is a 'small' loaf pan? My small could be your medium and so on! While much of this stuff is easy enough to google, it is nice to have it ready printed, so herewith some of the more common ones!

Volume		
1 cup	50 ml	
½ cup	125 ml	
⅓ cup	80 ml	
¼ cup	60 ml	4 tablespoons
1 tablespoon	15 ml	3 teaspoons
1 teaspoon	5 ml	
1 fluid ounce	30 ml	
1 US quart	950 ml	
Weight		
1 ounce	28 grams	
1 pound	16 ounces	454 grams
Length		
1 inch	2.54 centimetres	
1 foot	12 inches	30 centimetres

Volume-to-weight conversions

Since the volume measurement of an ingredient depends on how you pack the measuring cup/spoon and on the ingredient itself (how it is cut, its density, its water content), the volume-to-weight conversions are not absolute but they're close enough to use with confidence.

Dairy		
Cream	1 cup	240 grams
Cheese (hard, such as cheddar), grated	1 cup	100 grams
Cheese (fresh, such as crème fraîche/cream/cottage/ricotta)	1 cup	240 grams
Greek-style yoghurt	1 cup	250 grams
Milk	1 cup	240 ml
Parmesan cheese, grated	1 cup	110 grams

Nuts and seeds		
Almonds, shelled, whole	1 cup	140 grams
Almonds, shelled, roughly chopped	1 cup	100 grams
Almonds, sliced	1 cup	70 grams
Almond meal (aka almond flour or ground almonds)	1 cup	100 grams
Almond butter	1 cup	240 grams
Cashews, shelled, whole	1 cup	130 grams
Chia seeds	1 cup	160 grams
Coconut, unsweetened desiccated	1 cup	100 grams
Flax seeds	1 cup	150 grams
Hazelnuts, shelled, whole	1 cup	140 grams
Macadamia nuts, shelled, whole	1 cup	140 grams
Nut butter	1 cup	240 grams
Pistachios	1 cup	125 grams
Poppy seeds	1 cup	145 grams
Pumpkin seeds	1 cup	130 grams
Sesame butter	1 cup	240 grams
Sesame seeds	1 cup	150 grams
Sunflower seeds	1 cup	140 grams

Nuts and seeds (continued)		
Tahini (sesame butter)	1 tablespoon	18 grams
Walnuts, shelled, halves	1 cup	100 grams
Sugar and other sweeteners		
Agave syrup	⅓ cup	100 grams
Brown rice syrup	1 cup	300 grams
Honey	1 cup	300 grams
Honey	1 tablespoon	18 grams
Erythritol	1 cup	215 grams
Xylitol	1 cup	175 grams
Xylitol syrup	1 cup	300 grams
Molasses	1 cup	280 grams
Chocolate		
Cacao nibs	1 cup	120 grams
Chocolate, grated	1 cup	100 grams
Chocolate, roughly chopped	1 cup	120 grams
Cocoa powder	1 cup	120 grams
Fats and salt		
Butter	½ cup	120 grams
Butter	1 tablespoon	15 grams
Coconut oil	1 tablespoon	12 grams
Coconut oil	1 cup	200 grams
Salt, fine	1 teaspoon	5 grams
Salt, coarse	1 cup	220 grams
Salt flakes (e.g. Maldon salt)	1 tablespoon	10 grams

Fruit, vegetables, herbs

Baby spinach leaves	1 cup (packed)	30 grams
Basil	1 cup (packed)	20 grams
Blueberries	1 cup	190 grams
Carrots, grated	1 cup (loosely packed)	90 grams
Cauliflower florets	1 cup	85 grams
Parsley, finely chopped	1 cup	60 grams
Parsley	1 cup (loosely packed)	15 grams
Pomegranate seeds	1 cup	150 grams
Raspberries	1 cup	125 grams
Rocket	1 cup (packed)	25 grams
Shallots or onions, finely chopped	1 cup	120 grams
Strawberries	1 cup (small strawberries or large strawberries, sliced)	125 grams
Tomato paste	1 cup	300 grams

Other

Active dry yeast	1 teaspoon	5 grams
Active dry yeast vs. fresh yeast	1 gram active dry yeast	3 grams fresh yeast
Agar-agar	1 teaspoon	2 grams
Baking powder	1 standard sachet	11 grams or 1 tablespoon
Nutritional yeast	1 cup	60 grams
Psyllium husks	1 cup	80 grams
Tofu, silky	1 cup	255 grams

Pans and dishes

Springform and round tart or cake pan (diameter)

20 cm	8 inch/8.5-inch	
22/23 cm	9-inch	
25 cm	10-inch	

Square and rectangular cake pan or baking dish

20x20 cm	8x8-inch	
23x23 cm	9x9-inch	
25x25 cm	10x10-inch	
28x18 cm	11x7-inch	
22x33 cm	9x13-inch	

Loaf tin

20x10x6 cm	8x4x2.5 inch	
23x13x8 cm	9x5x3 inch	

Depths vary, so on this front the maths looks like this:		
6 cm	2½ inch	
8 cm	3 inch	
10 cm	4 inch	
A 'small' ramekin		
180 ml		

Temperature			
Degrees fahrenheit	Degrees celsius	Gas mark	Description
225	110	¼	Very slow
250	120/130	½	Very slow
275	140	1	Slow
300	150	2	Slow
325	160/170	3	Moderate
350	180	4	Moderate
375	190	5	Moderately hot
400	200	6	Moderately hot
425	220	7	Hot
450	230	8	Hot
475	240	9	Very hot

SOURCING INGREDIENTS

While it isn't overly difficult to find the majority of ingredients to produce low-carb goodies, the costs are not insignificant, and it helps to know where to get as much as possible at the best prices possible. There are the special spices and superfood ingredients that take a little more digging up, but which are worth having as they add so much flavour.

It's always cheaper to buy in bulk, so try to find somewhere you can source your nuts and seeds in bulk. Spices are likely to be fresher if you source them from stores that really specialise in them, so look for the Asian and Indian stores nearest to you for these.

In general, though, a good health shop is a great place to start as staff are usually very knowledgeable, so check out which stores are near to you. Chains like Wellness Warehouse, Dischem and Food Lover's Market have a pretty good footprint nationally, with an impressive array of products. Specialist organic and real food retailers are also out there, providing another channel you can use to source ingredients.

There are Banting and artisanal food markets popping up at a crazy rate, and these provide yet another source of not only pre-made products, but also basic ingredients like coconut or MCT oil, full-cream raw milk, etc. Hit google.co.za and you'll be amazed at what's out there.

The online universe gives you loads of sourcing options too, with a couple of local sites, such as:
www.absoluteorganix.co.za
www.healthmatrix.co.za
www.faithful-to-nature.co.za
www.goodlife.co.za
www.organicemporium.co.za
www.jacksonsrealfoodmarket.co.za
www.bantingbox.co.za
www.getbanting.co.za
These all offer a great selection of low-carb ingredients and finished goods.

There are also loads of sites, both local and international, where you can 'source' great grain-free, low-carb high-fat recipes and info on different ingredients. Go googling and an impressive array of sites will pop up. Reading broadly to get different opinions and testing these against your own experience is one of the most satisfying aspects of this journey. One of my favourite resources is www.marksdailyapple.com – while not a specific proponent of a low-carb high-fat diet, Mark Sisson offers balanced, intelligent and informed commentary on dietary issues that is accessible yet grounded in solid science.

The best resource at the end of the day, however, will be *you* and your will to find what you're looking for. Get active and search out local farmers for clean dairy, meat and veg, and pressure your local retailers to stock the stuff you need.

ACKNOWLEDGEMENTS

My thanks go to Jacana, and specifically to Bridget Impey, who took the proposal on board without hesitation. Special thanks to Kerrie Barlow for holding my hand through the production process, which, while not entirely foreign, was nevertheless a somewhat daunting challenge. She and her team made manifest what was in my mind.

Great thanks also go to my teams at gingko and Primal Chow, and in particular to Trecia Masilela, who has evolved into a pastry chef extraordinaire, and who has added much value throughout the tireless testing process.

To Taryne Jacobi, who handled the styling, and Michelle Wastie, our photographer, I am also grateful.

Lastly, I am deeply indebted to my sister whose belief in me and financial support has allowed me to develop the knowledge that is shared in this book.

PHOTO CAPTIONS

Endpapers: Hazelnuts in their shells
Page 1: Poppies at sunset
Page 3: Fresh raspberries in close up
Page 9: Harvesting coffee berries
Page 11: Whole, unmilled flax seeds
Page 25: Pastured bliss
Page 57: Field of flax in bloom
Page 73: Onions in bloom
Page 87: Field of sunflowers
Page 113: Almond trees in blossom
Page 133: Green coconut harvest
Page 149: Cranberry harvest on Canadian lakes
Page 161: Nature's patchwork quilt
Page 171: Ancient olive grove
Page 172: Cacao pods
Page 181: Getting to the heart of a lettuce
Page 191: A traditional spice tray in close up
Page 201: Dewy blueberries, just after harvesting

SELECT BIBLIOGRAPHY

Asprey, Dave, 2014, *The Bulletproof Diet*, Rodale: Emmaus, PA

Gottfried, Sara, 2013, *The Hormone Cure: Reclaim Balance, Sleep and Sex Drive; Lose Weight; Feel Focused, Vital, and Energized Naturally with the Gottfried Protocol*, Scribner: New York

Harari, Yuval Noah, 2011, *Sapiens: A Brief History of Humankind*, Harville Secker: London

Lustig, Robert, 2012, *Fat Chance: Beating the Odds Against Sugar, Processed Food, Obesity and Diet*, Penguin: New York

Minger, Denise, 2014, *Death by Food Pyramid: How Shoddy Science, Sketchy Politics and Shady Special Interests Have Ruined Our Health*, Primal Blueprint Publishing: Malibu, CA

Noakes, Prof Tim, Jonno Proudfoot and Sally-Ann Creed, 2013, *The Real Meal Revolution: The Radical, Sustainable Approach to Healthy Eating*, Quivertree Publications: Cape Town

Perlmutter, David, 2013, *Grain Brain: The Surprising Truth about Wheat, Carbs, and Sugar – Your Brain's Silent Killers*, Little Brown & Co: New York

Pollan, Michael, 2006, *The Omnivore's Dilemma: The Search for a Perfect Meal in a Fast-food World*, Penguin: London

Sisson, Mark, 2009, *The Primal Blueprint: Reprogramme your Genes for Effortless Weight Loss, Vibrant Health and Boundless Energy*, Vermilion: London

Taubes, Gary, 2007, *The Diet Delusion*, Random House Group: New York

Teicholz, Nina, 2014, *The Big Fat Surprise: Why Butter, Meat, and Cheese Belong in a Healthy Diet*, Simon & Schuster: London

Wolff, Rob, 2010, *The Paleo Solution: The Original Human Diet*, Victory Belt: Las Vegas

Various online sources including:
www.authoritynutrition.com
www.bulletproof.com
www.draxe.com
www.glycemicindex.com
www.jonbarron.org
www.livestrong.com
www.marksdailyapple.com
www.mercola.com
www.rebootedbody.com
www.whfoods.com (George Mateljan Foundation)
Youtube, Robert Lustig: "Sugar: The Bitter Truth"

ABOUT THE AUTHOR

Catherine Speedie is the owner of gingko, an organic and 'clean food'-oriented restaurant, bakery and catering business in Johannesburg. She is also the creator of Primal Chow, a brand dedicated to the world of Paleo and Banting goodies. A passionate traveller, Catherine brings flavours from all over the world into her cooking, believing strongly that food must be delicious and nutritious if it is to be fulfilling on all levels.

INDEX

Page numbers in bold indicate information about the ingredient in the Building a Banting Pantry section, pages 182 to 205.